# I Went to College for THIS?

## True Stuff about Life in the Business World—and How to Make Your Way Through It

Garrett Soden

PETERSON'S
Princeton, New Jersey

**Library of Congress Cataloging-in-Publication Data**

Soden, Garrett.

I went to college for this? / Garrett Soden.

p. cm.

Includes index.

ISBN 1-56079-339-2

1. Vocational guidance. 2. Corporate culture. 3. Managing your boss. 4. Interpersonal relations. 5. College graduates—Employment. I. Title.

HF5381.S643 1994

650.1—dc20 94-22155

CIP

Illustrations and hand lettering by Hal Mayforth.

Cover designed by Greg Wozney Design, Inc.

Printed in the United States of America

10 9 8 7 6 5 4 3 2 1

# Contents

# Acknowledgments

Although this book is a product of my own brain (so don't hold the demented parts against anyone but me), it would never have made it into a form to reach *your* brain without the help of a lot of people, beginning with Jim Gish, an editor with a clear vision of what should come next down the pike, and Andrea Pedolsky, my editor on this book—someone who not only accepted my somewhat weird writing style, but one who actually *encouraged* it. Peterson's and I are lucky to have editors like these.

My thanks also go out to everyone I talked to about their experiences on Planet Bizness, including Tom Harrison, Ed Seider, Hillary Jacobs, and Janice Ridenour, and all the others who preferred to remain anonymous. Others who weren't quoted but helped with general conversation and in other ways included Melanie Havens, Scott Ray, Dan Niebruggee, Nancy Niebrugge, Karen Ming, Megan Freeman, Gary Grundei, Marty Sweeney, Cheryl Fields, Jill Smolinski, Laurie Hunter, Debbie Wall, Jeff Book, and Bob Jacobs.

On the home front, I owe a great deal, as always to Denise K. Seider, for the whole deal love, encouragement, incisive insight, and a yank on the shirt every time I'm about to plunge over a cliff. Thanks also to Jordan, who was the first one to read the first paragraph of this manuscript and to pronounce it, "Not bad." And finally, thanks to Tom the Cat, my most consistent and accepting (if somewhat lackadaisical) supporter.

Introduction

# The World They Call Real—And Why You Need This Book to Tell You About It

Hey you—yeah, you with the college diploma. Come here a minute. Remember when you first started at Getcherdegree U and the professor in your first class said, "In this course we will be . . ." etc., and then she told you the stuff you'd be covering, how much finals counted for, and all that? And how it pretty much turned out to be the way she said?

O.K., now imagine you've just gotten a job. Somebody—probably a lot of people—will tell you what the deal is. Your boss will explain how "challenging" (they love that word) your assignments will be. The personnel department will give you the lowdown on hours, vacation, and so forth. The president might even shake your hand and tell you what a dynamic, innovative, progressive, [fill in the blank] company you now work for. You'll probably think, okay, so it's like in school. They tell you the deal and you do it. This is not sounding like an intense situation.

Attention All Young Jobsters: *They will not tell you the whole deal.* They can't, because they've lived too long in another world.

## Life on Planet Bizness

College and business—we're talking two completely different food chains, here. Check it out: in college, the professors are in control. Your history prof, for example, knows what he's going to teach. He teaches it to you and then he tests you to see if you learned it. He knows The Right Answer, and it's your job to learn it.

Not so with your boss, or anybody else in business. Nobody knows The Right Answer. When somebody thinks they've found it, somebody above them tells them it's wrong. Or something changes—market conditions, politics, the company's structure—and suddenly the answer *becomes* wrong. People lose face, money, or their job.

To thrive in such an environment, people in business resort to your basic human tribal behavior. They struggle as a group to find The Right Answer using their common knowledge, smarts, instinct, and folklore, the bits of which are in everyone's brain. President Carol has to count on what Vice President Earl knows about marketing; Earl has to count on what Director Melanie knows about packaging, and so forth, down to Bill in Shipping and Receiving. Together they hunt and gather, and if the business spirits are pleased they yield forth sustenance.

When the New One comes (that's you) the elders will try to explain it all, but it will be across a great cultural gap. They probably won't lie to you, but they might. What they will do are two things: they will speak in their own language, "Bizspeak," and they won't tell you the most basic information.

## Bizspeak Spoken Here

When I say Bizspeak, I'm not talking about terms like *liquid assets, current liabilities,* or *target market.* That's jargon, and every business has its own. I'm talking about the way bizpeople use language to cover up what they can't or don't want to talk about.

Let's take a simple example. Say you need some pencils. Your boss tells you that to get pencils, you have to fill out a Request for Pencils form, get it signed by the Purchasing Department, and give it to the Administrative Supplies department. You're thinking, these people must have a major problem. How can anybody get anything done if they have to go through all that just to get a pencil?

What your boss won't tell you is that *she* doesn't fill out that stupid form. She knows Neal in Administrative Supplies. She and Neal have a deal where Neal fills out the form and approves it on the spot and just sends the pencils. Your boss won't tell you not to fill out the form because that would be violating a strong tribal taboo, which is denying the power of this particular tribal ritual (filing out the form).

Here is where your boss uses Bizspeak. Instead of saying, "blow off the pencil form," she might say, "although procedure requires that you fill out a Request for Pencils form, you'll need to move more quickly on that front since I want you to get started today. See if you can't expedite your request by consulting with Neal in Supplies." Notice how much longer that took to say? That's typical.

Like any language, Bizspeak hides what its speakers are afraid of and celebrates what its culture values. But you don't know this when you start, so you don't realize that a "challenging" assignment probably means it's a pain, or that if a job requires a "detail-oriented" approach that means it's tedious and boring, or that "cost-effective" means cheap, or that "dynamic" means working like hell.

## What They Don't Tell You

All right, let's go back to when you started at Getcherdegree U. How would you describe your alma mater to a high school student who's thinking about going there? You'd tell her about the great poli sci department or a good philosophy prof that helped you out. You might say the chem lab was okay, the art department sucked, and that dorms weren't bad unless you get a Metallica fan next door like you had. You might talk about the town around it, the party atmosphere, the sports, the Greek system, and the keggers you went to. But what are you leaving out? *You're leaving out everything you had to adjust to so you could simply function in college—any college.*

Like what? Like registering for classes. Your high school buddy hasn't done that. Like picking a major. Like getting a meal ticket, or what to do if you can't stand your dorm mate, or how to drop or add a class, or work/study, or on-campus student jobs, or how to get used textbooks, or how to get your mail, or whether you can have a phone in your room. You would probably leave out that information for a few reasons.

First, because you learned it during your first year, and then you forgot about it. You took it for granted. Second, some of it was such a timesoak you'd rather not even remember it. And third, because that's not why you went to college. All that stuff is just stuff. But if you think back, it was confusing getting used to it the first time around.

That's the way it is in business. Bizpeople forget to tell you stuff for the same reasons: they take it for granted, they don't want to think about it, and it's just stuff—not the main deal.

Here are a few examples: bizpeople know when to talk to their boss about something and when it would be better to put it in a memo. If they put it in a memo, they'd know who to "cc," which stands for "carbon copy," even though carbon paper died around the time "I Like Ike" was the latest presidential campaign slogan. Do you know how to figure that out?

Would you know how to run a meeting that included your boss? Would you know how to prepare for a meeting with a hostile client? What about something as simple as lunch: in business, it matters how you spend that time. How can you find out what's expected of you?

The number of bizpeople who will sit you down and tell you all this is slightly more than zip. They're too busy. They assume you'll learn. And besides that, new kids do the darndest things when they jump in the pool, and it's fun to see who floats and who sucks *aqua*. It's an initiation thing.

But it's not just that they want to see you squirm. They just want to deal with the mundane stuff of business as little as possible so they can do the main part of business, which is getting things done—getting that client, selling those cough drops, servicing those retailers, or whatever. That's the fun part, and it's what you want to get to, too.

## What's in This Book, and Why You Need It

For the reasons I've just run down, your boss can't reveal all that stuff Bizspeak hides, and she probably doesn't even realize all the stuff she's leaving out. And yet, she wants you to figure all this out as soon as possible. Tomorrow would be nice.

Since *The Secret World of Everyday Office Workers* won't be on the next Oprah, I've written this book. In it, you'll find everything your boss wants you to know but can't tell you.

**Part One: Who You're Supposed to Know** focuses on your boss, your coworkers, clients, and vendors. Chapter 1, **Your Fearless Leader,** is about your boss. You should know that the secret stuff you have to learn never ends, especially when it comes to learning about what your boss wants. That can change depending on who's pushing her, and what needs to get done, or what kind of disaster just happened. I talked to managers who tell what they expect in a variety of situations, and what they see happen to the graduates who sign on to their cruise.

In Chapter 2, **The Cubes Next Door: Coworkers,** you'll learn how to figure out who all those nice people staring at you from across the aisle are and what you should do about it. Notice yet another big difference here between school and work: in the office, you're *always* working with someone else to get something done. Even if you work on a part of it alone, someone else will give you info, or get info from you, or approve what you're doing, or ask you to check what they're doing, or in some other way muck around with you and your stuff. You've got to be good at the work, but you've also got to do the political thing. Break out *The Prince* if you feel the need, but this chapter covers some predicaments Machiavelli would have thrown up his hands at.

Another difference between school and work is that in the office it's about money. And people get weird about money. We cover that in Chapter 3, **Clients and Other Money People,** where you'll hear about how you've got to deal with money people. Don't think that it's as easy as always doing what the client wants.

In **Part Two: What You're Supposed to Do,** we get real specific about all the stuff you didn't realize you had to do when you got a job but is the stuff you actually will spend tons of time doing. Like meetings. Like paperwork. Like figuring out when you're going to do what you thought you were hired to do.

Chapter 4, **In Your Face: The First Weeks,** is a guide to those just beamed on deck. You'll learn how to figure out who's got the power, who *thinks* they have the power; who will be happy to answer your stupid questions and who won't, and what to do during lunch time (if you think the answer is just "eat lunch" you haven't been paying attention).

On to meetings, covered in Chapter 5, **Meetings: Get a Clue.** You've been in meetings before, but not like these. There's maneuvering going on. Dour looks and sidelong glances. What does it all mean? When do you jump in, when do you hang back? We'll cover all that, give you a way to guess what's going to go on in a meeting before you get there and a way to size up who wants what once you're in there.

Paperwork. Gotta love it. Chapter 6, **Trekking the Paper Trail,** lets you know how you can sniff out essential paperwork from what you can probably blow off. But we also cover the rest of the paper blizzard—how bizfolks use paper to push their ideas, get people lined up on their side, and, that perennial favorite, how they use it to cover their ass. Stop that snickering—there comes a time when we all need some cover.

In Chapter 7, **Smells Like Team Spirit: Corporate Culture,** you'll learn how to figure out the unspoken mores of your new world. A lot of this depends on what all companies have in common—the hierarchy—who pushes who how far, and what effect this has on their mood. We'll explore some of the more pithy things that have been observed about hierarchies, and then move in close to show you what you can learn about your particular company's culture.

**Part Three, Where You're Supposed to Get To,** covers power, *Power,* POWER! How to wield it to crush your opponent until he begs for—not really. But you do need to know a few things. Chapter 8, **Who's Got the Power,** expands on the first scoping you did when you arrived. You'll learn how to read an organizational chart. Not just what's there, but what ain't there. ("Say, how is it that Ed is officially a manager, but nobody reports to him?") You'll also learn to see where you fit, not according to the chart, but according to where you might want to be.

Next up we've got Chapter 9, **What You've Got and What You're Supposed to Want.** Here you'll learn how the whole enchilada (as in I'll take that with green salary on the side and a cheesy health plan) of a typical compensation package is put together in the bizworld. I'll also reveal all the hidden perks that come with most paper-pushin' jobs.

We'll also look at what your company would like you to aspire to, with a few tests to see if it's what *you* want to aspire to. If you're good, business pretty much knows only two ways to reward you: money and power. While more money is almost always good, and power means you can put up a Smashing Pumpkins poster and no one can tell you not to (remember, it'll be retro by then), you shouldn't always go for that promotion. You need to decide what you actually want to *do.* Although the company doesn't always know it, it has other stuff it could give you—a chance to change departments and learn a completely different job, for example, or the chance to head your own project, like putting Smashing Pumpkins–brand granola bars on the market.

Finally, in Chapter 10, **Satisfaction: The Work and Life Thing,** we *escutcheon y repetin:* Life is not all work. You're thinking, yeah, like I could forget *that.* But it happens. Look around. Notice how your coworkers think that shipment of flanges to Milwaukee is *really important.* Seems incredible, but they didn't always think that. They're just getting into the gestalt of business, which is more than flanges. They're thinking of that guy in Milwaukee waiting for his flange. It's important to him, so it's important to them. The trick is to be balanced; to know how much of the company's ethos you should let seep into your groundwater. On the other *mano,* don't think your "entry level position" is just a McJob, or it will be. And don't expect work to fill all your psychic requirements.

Now let me tell you what's not in this book. There is no advice about how to get a job. There are plenty of books about that. There is no advice about specific business skills like writing, budgeting, or firing your best friend. There are no speeches about How Great It Is To Work In Business And Live The American Dream. Sometimes it actually *is* great, but you have to find that out for yourself.

## How to Use This Book

Read it.

# PART 1

# Who You're Supposed to Know

Chapter 1

# Your Fearless Leader

YOUR BOSS. THE PERSON WHO BOSSES YOU. FROM THE START, THIS RELATIONSHIP IS DIFFERENT FROM ALL OTHERS IN LIFE. EVEN IF YOU'VE HAD A BOSS BEFORE IN SOME OTHER JOB, THIS WILL BE DIFFERENT BECAUSE NOW YOU'RE WORKING IN A JOB THAT'LL BE PART OF YOUR CAREER. YOU'LL HAVE STRONGER OPINIONS ABOUT HOW TO DO YOUR JOB THAN YOU DID ABOUT DELIVERING PIZZAS.

Not only is the relationship different from any you've had before, it's going to be different depending on your boss. One boss might want to be your dad, another might want to be your lord and master, another might want to be your best friend. Clear all that from your mind, because no matter what your boss says, there's one main thing that your boss is supposed to do with you: make you valuable to the company. A smart boss knows that if you love your work, you'll be more valuable to the company—but not all bosses are smart. And even if they want you to love your job, they can't always set it up that way. There will always be stuff that nobody wants to do but that needs to get done, and being the new addition to the company guess who's going to have to do it? It's your boss's job to get you to do it and to like it, if he can.

## Catalog o' Bosses

The very idea of a boss is a strange thing. In business, becoming a boss is what confirms your value. The reasoning goes that to get promoted to boss you've shown that not only are you smart enough to know what you should do, you're smart enough to know what *other people* should do. At its core, this idea is an odd, artificial way for humans to relate to each other. And people who become bosses react to it in strange ways.

Some are embarrassed by it and try to deny their power by never telling their employees what to do. Some revel in it, thinking that a combination of divine anointment and natural selection has resulted in their right to order you around. Most bosses just try to live with it and are at times uncomfortable and at other times satisfied by it.

All this angst means that bosses spend a lot of time searching for a way to feel good about what they do. Just like every rock singer in Seattle wants to be the next Eddie Vedder, every boss wants to be the next Tom Peters (the guy who wrote *In Search of Excellence* and several other business books). No big surprise: ninety-nine percent of them aren't. So if you've spent any time reading management books and think that's how most bosses are, forget it. That's how they *want* to be—and how they want you to see them. But how they really are is the way most of us are: we have a cherished picture of ourselves accomplishing great things, but mostly we sit around and watch too much TV.

On top of that, most bosses didn't become bosses because they have an inborn ability to manage people. That's not how they got to be boss. Usually it's because they worked hard, were loyal to the company, did what *their* boss told them, had good skills, kissed ass, got an MBA, or started the company. None of these things have much to do with supervising employees.

You're saying what about that MBA? Don't they teach *management* in business school, for God's sake? Well, yeah, but here's what psych professors Mardy Grothe and Peter Wylie from Columbia University have to say about that in their book *Problem Bosses* (Facts on File):

> In our view, when it comes to solving the problem of problem bosses, MBA programs don't help much. First, 99.9 percent of the bosses of the world never set foot inside them, so whatever gets taught in these schools is inaccessible to most bosses. Second, while business schools often provide excellent training in areas like accounting or finance, they're weak in the area of managing people. We've examined the curricula of some of the best business schools in the country. What little they offer in this area is so theoretical and abstract that it's almost useless. Although courses on "Human Resources Management" may have some sensitizing value, they don't train prospective bosses how to deal with employees.

There's an inherent conflict in being a boss. Although you're supposed to manage people, you're supposed to care about the company. Some bosses learn that caring about people can be the means to the end of caring about the company. That's what all the management books say. But too many bosses get squeezed in the day-to-day pressure to perform, and they panic. That's when they don't give a damn what you think and just tell you to do your job. Don't get too self-righteous about all this—most of us would do the same thing, and there's a good chance you will someday.

To cope, bosses cop a million different attitudes. Some books on management try to nail down the different types of bosses into stereotypes. This method is supposed to make them easier to handle. You check out your boss, read your book, and say, "Oh, this guy is a Manipulator to the max." Then you read all about what a Manipulator is and does, and supposedly you know how to react to your boss's every whim. But then you check him out a little more, read more, and then say, "Wait a sec. Maybe he's not a Manipulator. He's sounding more like a Street Fighter." So you follow the advice the book has for *that* kind of boss.

Here are a few ways bosses are described: The Nice Guy, the Panic Button Boss, the Commandant, the Petty Bureaucrat, the Passed-Over, the Craftsman, The Jungle Fighter, the Company Man, the Gamesman, the Heel Grinder, the Egotist, the Incompetent, the Slob, the Dramatic, the Paranoid, the Depressive, the Compulsive, the Schizoid, the Innovator, the Expert, the Helper, the Defender, the Self-Developer, the Evangelist, the Product Champion, the Executive Champion, the Godfather, the Workaholic, the Shark, and simply, the Jerk.

You don't expect me to pass up a chance to give you my list, do you? Here it is:

**The Micromanager** This guy has to control everything you do, in as much detail as possible. He'll want to approve every move you make. A Micromanager anywhere in the chain above you can cause trouble. I once had a boss whose boss was a Micromanager. This guy was a vice president, yet he wanted to pick out the color of paper I used for a flyer. There isn't a lot you can do if you have a Micromanager for a boss, but you can use a few techniques to help you from going crazy.

The first is to give up. Let him make all the decisions. Ask him about even the smallest detail of your job, and what he thinks you should do. At some point, you'll reach his limit, and he'll tell you to make decisions for yourself. Don't fool yourself into thinking that you'll be able to make all decisions—all you've done is to begin to get a feel for the level at which he might tolerate your having some control. Next time, try and make that decision without asking him, and see how it goes. Flatter him. Tell him you didn't think it was worth his time, and that since he'd asked you to make a similar decision before, you thought it would be okay. After a while, you should be able to figure out the range in which he'll allow you to work.

**The Touchy-Feely Boss** This boss read *I'm Okay, You're Okay* one too many times. She needs to be loved. She hates the idea that she has power over you, so instead of telling you what to do she lets you guess by trying to read her signals. These can be pretty subtle. It's a dangerous game, because you might be cruising through your job thinking *no problem* when suddenly she calls you into her office. She might act disappointed in you, and eventually she'll get around to what her expectations were, and how you failed to meet them. Getting along with this kind of boss is actually pretty easy. Just ask her what she wants you to do. And then repeat back what you think she said, and ask her if that's right. This technique cuts through the muck because after a while she'll get tired of thinking of cloudy ways to tell you what to do and will just *tell* you.

**The Task Master** This kind of boss just cares about getting the job done. Period. You can leave all the friendly chatting behind and forget about worrying if she likes you or hates you. What makes a Task Master happy is when you get a lot of work done in a little bit of time. She's not that big on creative thinking. She doesn't want you to ruminate or brainstorm over stuff. To her, that's downtime. The good thing about a Task Master is you always know where you stand. Did you get out those five letters, make those phone calls, and review that contract? Okay, she likes you today. Slack off, and you're dog meat.

**The One Minute Maniac** I actually wrote a whole book on this guy (a humor book, but unfortunately it described some bosses that are really out there), entitled *The One Minute Maniac*. He's someone who thinks he can control his subordinates by devoting about two percent of his time to totally phony strokes and slams. As in, "Jenkins, you're doing a *really fine* job here," or "Jenkins, I'm *really disappointed* in your performance." This guy would sell you to the Klingons for nine bucks if he thought the company would make a profit. The best way to deal with this kind of boss: don't trust him.

You can make up your own boss system. Try using music categories: the Country Western boss, the Grunge boss, the Hip-Hop boss, the Metal boss. Works as well as anything else. Stupid as it sounds, any time you spend at this game will actually be well spent because you'll probably come up with an insight you didn't have before.

But the truth is that all these stereotypes, mine, yours, and everybody else's, are just that—stereotypes. It's all an attempt to get a hold on something impossible to get a hold on. Your particular boss will be a mixture of these qualities. It's not that these descriptions don't have value—you can learn a lot by reading them or making them up—just don't buy any one of them completely. Remember a very simple fact: your boss is a human, hard as that may be to believe sometimes.

## What Your Boss Is Worried About

So if you can't sort bosses into categories, how can you figure out why they do what they do? Let's start with your attitude, the way you might think about your boss without even knowing it.

The first thing you'll probably do is react to your boss the way you've reacted to the other authority figures in your life. But there are some real differences here. Although it might first seem like it, your boss is not like your professor or your parents. Your professor wanted *you* to learn the subject. The goal of your college was to educate *you.* That's what the institution does. Your parents, no matter how much you fought with them, were trying to talk *you* into stuff they thought was good for *you.* In both of these cases, the whole deal was to make things better for *you.* (Notice how I keep italicizing the word *you?* That's so *you* get it. In school and with your parents, everything was about *you.)*

But business ain't about you. In business, the goal is not to educate you, or improve you, or really, to do anything for you. The goal is to make money. Making you happy is, with luck, a by-product. So your boss can only be concerned with you up to a certain point.

Instead, your boss is concerned with *her* boss. If your boss is a supervisor, she's thinking about *her* boss, the director. If your boss is a v.p., he's thinking about the prez. What if your boss is the prez? Then she's thinking about her board of directors.

What's on her mind is the same sort of things that are on your mind, except at a different level. She's got assignments she's trying to carry out; if she's the prez, the board of directors may have told her to make a certain division profitable by a certain date—or else. At the same time, she's probably working on a pet project of her own, something perhaps no one else in the company believes in. Now you come along. You might be a big help or a big pain, but either way you're not the main concern.

Bosses are stuck in the middle. Not only do they have to worry about their bosses, they have to worry about their underlings. If you look at it that way, you realize they have less control over their job than you do because there is always somebody under them who can screw things up. One manager put it this way, "There are so many things out of my control, yet I'm responsible for them."

As long as you remember that your boss isn't your dad or your prof, you'll be okay, and you can be open to the good part of having a boss. First of all, the boss will take more heat than you. If you make a suggestion, and it's lame but your boss lets you to do it anyway, it's his problem. And secondly, if you've got a cool boss who cares about you (and while a boss can't care about you to the detriment of the company, he can still care about you), then you can actually have fun at work. Your boss can protect you from busywork, give you interesting stuff to do, promote you, give you a raise, talk you up to other managers—in short, be your champ.

## What Your Boss Will Make You Do

A lot of grunt work. This can't be helped. Everybody goes through it no matter who they are, no matter what school they went to, no matter how impressive their degree, and no matter how smart or talented they are. Someone I'll call Clarence still remembers one of his early bosses, and how he resisted him:

> I had a boss who just drove me nuts. He just hounded me all the time about the most stupid, trivial things that didn't matter to the business. My reaction was to ignore him. Well, it was so stupid. I mean, I could have made him happy—and he would have left me alone—if, for the first few times he asked me all these little things, I'd just answer him. If I'd just done what he asked in the beginning, he would have gone away.

So the first thing to remember when your boss gives you a crappy job is that it's just part of the system. It's nothing personal. You might have a boss who will take the time to explain why every little job she gives you needs to get done, but it's more likely that you'll get one that won't. Most bosses don't have the time to hold your hand. Clarence went through agony with his earlier bosses, but that doesn't make him especially sympathetic to the graduates who now come to work for him:

> I see a lot of MBAs from fancy-schmancy schools come in with a real attitude that they shouldn't have to do this work. They've been led to believe in their classes in college that they'll be able to go out in the working world and be the most valuable people on earth. They don't realize that all of us do a lot of grunt work every day and that it's part of the job. As a boss, you have to spend a lot of time just knocking them down a notch or two, and explaining, "Look, I stay here and do this work—you're gonna stay here and do this work. And if you want to go and find a better job, go find it."

Some do, and others stick it out. How do the ones who stay learn to stand it?

> The ones who stay? They get it. I don't really know what happens. To tell you the truth, I think the people whom they work for don't really care. I don't really care if they get it or not. I don't spend a lot of time explaining it to them. And no one will.

Let's take a look at the type of work I'm talking about. Here's something that happened to one worker I'll call Lupé when she had just started her advertising career:

> At four o'clock in the afternoon my airline client calls me up and says there's a fare war going on and we're going to put out ads in the top 50 news-

> papers—and every single one's going to have a different price. We're going to have 200 cities in every ad, and every ad is going to have 200 different prices. Now here's a list of all the prices in alphabetical order, but we want them in monetary order—all the cities that cost $49 to fly to, all the cities that cost $59—for 200 ads. Make sure you don't miss a one because it would cost the company an unbelievable amount of money if they had to refund everyone ten bucks.

Talk about tedious. But here's the thing: who else is going to do a job like that? You don't need a degree to put prices together—a secretary could do it. But Lupé wisely didn't pawn it off to a secretary for good reason. A secretary doesn't get paid enough to take responsibility for a job with stakes that are that high. What if the secretary made a mistake? What would Lupé say to her boss? "It wasn't my fault! Clarissa messed up!" Lupé's boss would predictably respond, "But it was your responsibility. Clarissa I talk to. You I fire."

Earning your degree didn't just teach you the information you learned; it taught you how to maintain the drive you need to persist where others dropped out; how to get the details that others miss. It's *that* quality that your boss will be counting on in a lot of your early assignments.

Another reason a boss will make you do certain kinds of work is that a boss is responsible for money the company spends, and your time is cheaper. Lupé tells of a time when she told a subordinate to wait for a TV commercial on videotape to be finished and then get it to the client:

> I said, "Look, this videotape isn't ready, it's not going to be ready until ten o'clock tonight. You're going to stay here and wait for it. You're going to play it. You're going to drive two hours to deliver it." His response was, "You're out of your mind, I've got a date tonight." I said, "No, I'm not out of

my mind. I bill out at $250 an hour, and you bill out at $25 an hour. You're staying." He might've thought, "Well, I went to Harvard Business School, I shouldn't have to sit here." And I'm thinking, "Well, yes you should. This is how advertising is made. This is how a company makes money."

The flip side of this is that as long as you understand why you have to put up with this most of the time, your boss (if he's at all reasonable) will understand when you can't. Lupé gives an example of how this works for her:

> Let's say one of my employees comes to me and says, "You know what, it's my daughter's birthday tonight, and I just can't miss it." Quite often I'll say, "Oh, I'm glad you told me, it's no big deal, if it's your daughter's birthday I'll stay here and get things done."

When you get really bummed about all the crap you have to do and you start mouthing off about how you didn't take out a forty-thousand-dollar student loan so you could wind up making copies of faxes because your boss doesn't like the curly paper, keep one thing in mind: this is where you *are,* not where you're going. Because you've got the sheepskin, you *are* going somewhere. A lot of people around you aren't. Hillary Jacobs learned this during a summer job she had where she was coding surveys:

> It wasn't very scintillating work. And at the beginning I was really spending a lot of time bitching about it. "God, this is so *boring!*" But I was working in a big group of people. And one time my boss took me aside and said, "Hillary, you're going back to Harvard in the fall. You may be bored by this, but you're working with people who are doing this and they're not going anyplace else—you better

> snap out of it." It was really something for me to say, "Oh. Yeah. Sorry."

So be cool, and be patient.

## Mood Swings R Us, or Stop That Cringing

Bosses have both long-term pressure and short-term pressure. Short-term pressure, whether it's from the job or any other part of their life, can make 'em moody. Like when your boss's boss calls him up and asks where the hell the Sludge-B-Gone marketing report is. Your boss gets nervous and calls you. He may or may not tell you he's getting leaned on. All you know is you've got to jump.

Moods are damn powerful things. If your boss seems completely torqued today, wait until tomorrow before you decide what to do. It might pass. Or, if your boss just scored a major win on something and is psyched, that's the time to ask for something.

Sometimes you'll see a pattern to your boss's moods—a sort of PMS for bosses, either male or female. It could be that at the end of every quarter they have to review their budgets and get cranky. Or it might seem to have no outside trigger. I once had a boss who would spend a week picking on one of her subordinates while everybody else got a free ride. Next week it would be someone else. We used to sit around and guess who the next unlucky soul would be. When it came around to your turn, you just put up with it until she moved on, and that's the way it was.

All this seems obvious, but with the professional nonstick coating everybody in business walks around with, sometimes it's hard to remember that inside your boss is a hunka-hunka churning emotion—just like you.

And speaking of your hunka-hunka churning emotion, remember that while you've got to move like the gentle breeze when your boss is touchy, she's not going to do the same for you (unless she knows that your pet ferret died or something). In most cases, if you're ready to flush the Sludge-B-Gone account and the horse it rode in on, that's tough for you. She'll expect you to be in there hammering on it, come hell or high water.

## How to Serve Your Fearless Leader

You're thinking, "I need *you* to tell me how to do what my boss wants me to do? *Hello?* How about if I just do what my boss *tells me* to do?" Ah, but it's never that simple. Why? Because, again, unlike your parents or your professors, *your boss has almost no idea how much work you have to do.*

Your parents told you what to do. They knew how long it took to clean out the garage. They knew when you said you couldn't find the broom and that's why it took so long that you were full of it. Your professors also knew your work better than you. They made it up. They did it year after year. They knew *exactly* how long it should take a student to do the reading, write the paper, and take the test.

Not so your boss. Oh, he'll know how long it takes to do some things, especially your early assignments. He's probably done them himself. But they will be mixed with jobs he hasn't done. The more independent you become, the more your boss will keep throwing work at you. The more of it you do, the more of it he'll give to you. In the working world, this isn't torture—it's a compliment. "Bosses think, 'Well, she's done such a good job, I'll just keep giving her more work,'" says one boss. If you get overloaded and don't tell your boss, it's your problem. Look at it this way:

**In School, You *Can't* Dodge Work But You Can Shift Deadlines** You've got to do what the professor assigns, period, because there's a certain amount of course work to get through to earn your degree. Due dates, though, can be changed depending on how the professor feels.

**At Work, You *Can* Dodge Work But You *Can't* Shift Deadlines** Many times if you make a convincing case to your boss that you're overloaded, she'll give the job to someone else. But deadlines are different. Says one worker I talked to:

> In college, yeah, there are deadlines, but there's no *real* deadline. If you go to your professor and say, "I was up half the night, blah, blah, blah, blah, I couldn't study for this test," usually they'll give you a later date. Well, you know, in business, there *is* a deadline. It's either done or it isn't. You may not even get paid if you don't do it on time.

So what do you do? Here are a few tips, many of them shamelessly stolen from Tom Harrison, a young senior v.p. at a public relations company (thanks, Tom):

• KNOW YOUR BOSS'S LIKES AND DISLIKES • We're not talking about how your boss likes it when you show up on time. All bosses like that. We're talking does he like to get information in memos or phone calls? Does she only want to see the final version of something, or does she want to see all the drafts? What's his style? Try asking one of your compadres who's worked for your boss for a while.

• KNOW YOUR BOSS'S BOSS'S LIKES AND DISLIKES • That way you can know what your boss is trying to do, even if she uses a different style. If her boss wants to see a lot of choices, your boss may have you work on projects she knows will never be picked for final approval. That may be frustrating as hell unless you realize that your boss has to have you do it to please her boss.

• AIM AT YOUR BOSS'S OBJECTIVES • That's different from doing the job you're asked to do. Your boss might tell you to compile the mailing list for the Western region, which you could do easily. But the computer guy told you that a new list would be ready in a few days. Don't just compile the old one, thinking that that's what you were told to do. Think about the bigger objective your boss is trying to accomplish. She's not trying to compile a mailing list—she's trying to sell widgets (or whatever). It might be more important that you wait and get the new list instead of slavishly following her instructions. Ask your boss. Let her make the decision. When you get in the habit of this, you'll be part of the process instead of just a grunt, and your boss will start to ask what you think should be done on the Smithers account.

• DON'T SURPRISE YOUR BOSS • They *really hate* that. Tell him what's going on. Don't try to protect him from bad news. He'll be twice as pissed if he finds out you knew about a disaster and didn't tell him right away. If you know you can fix it before it becomes a problem, fine; otherwise tell him.

Don't try to surprise your boss with good news, either—like working for weeks trying to bring in a new client without letting your boss know you're doing it. Your boss might call up the client and say, "So, Fred, how about if I send young Roger over there to show you some of our new services?" To which Fred replies, "Young Roger's been here three times in the last week." When your boss hangs up Fred thinks he's an idiot because he doesn't know what his staff is doing. Your boss, meanwhile, begins a slow burn.

• DON'T BRING YOUR BOSS A PROBLEM UNLESS YOU HAVE AT LEAST A DIM IDEA OF A SOLUTION • If you just drop bombs in your boss's lap, you're teaching her to look at you and think, "Here comes trouble." She'll also think you're too stupid to think for yourself, and in business this is generally considered an undesirable quality. So take a shot at suggesting something, even if you don't have much of a clue. Something like, "The computer just ate the HandiFan catalog text file. Would it be possible to get the original on disk from Hank at HandiFan?" Very rarely will a boss say, "What are you, insane? Don't ever try to tell me what to do!" Usually a boss will appreciate that you tried, even if you are insane. After a while your suggestions will get better, but you've got to start somewhere—so, practice.

• PUT IT IN WRITING • Don't try to keep things in your head. Write it down. That way you can show your boss rather than rattle off details that she'll have to write down. (More about this in Chapter 6, *Trekking the Paper Trail.*)

• BE POSITIVE • Yep, that's right. Look on the bright side. Have a cheery smile. Nobody likes a smart-ass, cynical kid who thinks the "American Way of Business" is a pile. If you think so, what are you doing in the thick of it? You will definitely run into stuff you hate—bureaucracy, time-wasting, bad politics, all of it. That's not just business—that's life. You can snivel about it or you can rise above it and get something done.

The final point here: your boss does not want just a worker bee. You didn't need to go to college to be that. Your boss wants somebody who can think. Tom Harrison puts it like this:

> Your skills are important to get into a job, but understanding is vital to your long-term success. Skills change, but the ability to think analytically, to create strategically, and to communicate persuasively will be the keys to your success.

## Excuse Me, Sir, But Wasn't That a Gigantic Blunder?

Sometimes bosses are wrong. *(Whoa! You're kidding!)* And sometimes you gotta tell them. And sometimes you better not. And sometimes you have to tell somebody else.

**When to Tell Them** Most of the time, if you think you've got a better way to do something, or you think your boss's way will cause damage, you can tell her without a problem. As long as you're suggesting and not insisting, your boss will probably be glad for the extra brain power. Just don't get obnoxious about it. That's like being a back seat driver.
Things not to do when disagreeing with your boss:

• DON'T MAKE IT A SHOWDOWN • Don't say, "If we do that it'll ruin everything!" Do I need to be telling you this? It's sort of obvious that you shouldn't insult your boss to her face.

• DON'T DISAGREE IN FRONT OF OTHERS • Wait until you can talk to your boss one-on-one. If your boss tells you the plan in a meeting, just nod your head. Later you can corner him and make your point.

If he asks you what you think in a meeting, go ahead and say what's on your mind, unless it's really, really bad. In that case, just say you have some reservations about it and that you'd like to get some more facts and discuss it with him later.

• DON'T POUT • If your boss tells you to do it her way, don't go out and tell all your coworkers how your boss wouldn't know a good idea if it bit her. That kind of talk will come back and bite *you.*

• DON'T GO OVER YOUR BOSS'S HEAD • If you do, here's what

will happen. You tell Mr. Moe that your boss, Mr. Curly, done you wrong. Moe says, "I'll look into it." Moe talks to Curly. Curly says, "Why that little pip-squeak! I'll murdalize her!" The only time you want to do this is when there's something *really wrong,* which we discuss below.

**When Not to Tell Them** If you're always disagreeing with your boss, you're going to have to bite your tongue most of the time. And frankly, if you hate your boss and want to see him screw up and hope he gets fired, then obviously don't let him ride on your smarts. Just make sure you're not riding shotgun when he crashes and burns.

And don't tell your boss if there's a problem that's way serious: stealing from the company, sexually harassing people, getting high on company time, hiring or firing people on account of race or religion—you know, the big ugly things. In any of these cases, go to your friend in the personnel department. (You don't have a friend in the personnel department? Read Chapter 2, where I explain why you should have one.)

**When to Tell Someone Else** As just mentioned—the big ugly things. If your boss is a druggie or hitting on you five times a day, don't try to work it out with him. You've got to bust him. Go directly to the personnel department and tell them what's going on.

If you're a real gambler and you're having problems with your boss that aren't the big ugly kind but may drive you nuts anyway, you can try what I just told you *not* to do: going over your boss's head. Sometimes Mr. Moe will say, "Why, I'll murdalize him!" and thank you for telling him.

Or you might want to try to get a buzz going among everybody else at the company so that the general perception is that your boss is a buckethead. Next thing you know, someone above your boss promotes you to a level equal to your boss. Be advised, though. Both these strategies are sort of like rollerblading down a steep hill. If you can keep your balance, it's a kick; if you can't, somebody will be scraping you off the pavement.

## How to Do What *You* Want to Do

After everything I've already said, you may be thinking, "So when do I get to do anything I want to do?" You might think the only way is to put up with dogwork for years until you become president. Not so. You have to look for openings, and the trick is to realize that they don't *look* like openings. Here are a few:

**The Stressed-Out Boss Opening** If you know what your boss is stressed out about, sometimes you can figure out something cool that you'd like to do that would help her at the same time. Don't suggest something you'll hate just to try to help. You'll do a cruddy job and feel bummed that you volunteered. But let's say you want to use the new software that makes charts. You might say, "What if I put some charts together that showed how Sludge-B-Gone is wiping its nearest competitor, Scum-Away, away?" If she says yes, you get to do something cool and score points at the same time.

**The Overload of Work Opening** Earlier I said that if your boss gives you too much work, you should say so. When you do this, you can try to tweak your assignments so they're a little closer to what you like. Think of your to-do list as a menu. What do you think you can do best? What would you like doing the most? Sort that out, and then go to your boss and say, "I've got more than I can do. I'd like to work on these projects because they're right down my alley. What can we work out about the other stuff?" Remember that telling your boss which assignments you like is a plus. She'll figure you'll work hard on the assignments you want to do and she won't have to hound you about them all the time. This trick ain't sure-fire, but it'll work more often than you think.

**The Extra Work Opening** You can always just ask to put more stuff on your list. Obviously, make it stuff you want to do. If you do a good job, what often happens is your boss starts to think this extra project you've got going is important. She starts to think, "Yeah, that's the ticket." And so the next time you tell her you're overloaded she keeps you on your pet project and lets you unload the scuzwork.

**The It's Not My Department Opening** There's often work that doesn't fall neatly into anyone's bailiwick. Sometimes people fight hard not to take it. Sometimes they're fighting not because the project is boring but simply because they're power-tripping. Sometimes it's because they think they don't know anything about it and are afraid they'll fail. It's a great time for you to step in and kick it. This is probably the most common opportunity to write your own ticket, because most people are just too plain scared to step outside their job description.

To sum up: just doing what you're told won't make you very happy or get you very far up the ladder. The secret is to invent a project you know you can do well—whether or not it's in your area of expertise—and then convince your boss and anyone else who will listen that it will work and that you're the one to do it.

## Chapter 2

# The Cubes Next Door: Coworkers

IN THE PREVIOUS CHAPTER ABOUT BOSSES, I TOLD YOU THAT YOU HAVE TO CHUCK THE MODELS OF AUTHORITY THAT ARE FLOATING AROUND IN YOUR HEAD: KID/PARENT AND STUDENT/TEACHER. THAT APPLIES NOT ONLY TO YOU AND YOUR BOSS BUT TO YOU AND THE OTHER PEOPLE YOU WORK WITH.

It's easy to think of yourself as a kid or a student with anybody who's older at work, even if they are below you in the power pyramid. This can lead to laughable mistakes. Tom Harrison remembers how it was when he first got a job:

> On my first day of work my secretary gave me something to proofread. I proofread the thing and I thought, "She left out two paragraphs, but she must have done it on purpose because she's been here a lot longer than I have." And I almost didn't tell her. And when I told her, she said, "Oh, thank you so much!" She would have been killed and I would have been responsible for letting it go by.

> But I thought, "I can't question her, she's older than I am." For the first few weeks I was even asking her for permission on when I could go home.

You can also feel second-rate if you're surrounded by MBAs and all you've got is a bachelor's degree. Don't let it throw you. People in business know that who you are is more important than what degree you have. Here's what Mark McCormack says about MBAs in *What They Don't Teach You at Harvard Business School* (Bantam):

> What I discovered was that a master's in business can sometimes block an ability to master experience. Many of the early MBAs we hired were either congenitally naive or victims of their business training. The result was a kind of real-life learning disability—a failure to read people properly or to size up situations and an uncanny knack for forming the wrong perceptions . . . . To assume, as I once did, that advanced degrees or high IQ scores automatically equal "business smarts" has often proved an expensive error in judgment.

(If you've got an MBA, don't take offense. I'm sure he didn't mean you. You're much too bright to let your degree hang you up.)

No matter what degree you have, when you first get a job you feel like everybody else knows what's going on but you're hopelessly out of it. That's just because everybody else knows what's going on and you *are* out of it—but not hopelessly. You're not expected to know much when you start, so don't compare yourself to somebody who's been there ten years, or even one year. Don't even compare yourself to what you think of yourself. "When I was first hired out of college," Tom Harrison says, "my boss looked at me and said, 'All right, I'll tell you what. You can't write, but we think we can teach you.' I walked in thinking the *only* thing I could do was write. Now

I'm thinking, 'Why would they hire me if the only thing I thought I could do I can't do?'"

Your boss knows that you don't know what you're doing, so relax. If you need a trick to psych yourself up, try inventing the reputation you'd like to get among your coworkers. Imagine that everybody sees you as the new kid who's got a lot to learn but has tremendous potential. Picture people talking about you. "That's Fergeson. New, but very sharp." You need to get your mind in the space between being intimidated and being arrogant. You might call it "humble confidence" or "modest self-assurance." You've got to get stable in your attitude so you can move on to the real game: getting to know the players, sizing them up, and getting sized up by them.

## Who You Should Get to Know

You should get to know everybody you might work with in any capacity at any time while you're at that company. That may be a lot of people, but the more people you know, the better. So start from day one.

On that first day somebody will take you around and introduce you to a bunch of people. You'll get their names, ranks, and serial numbers. This won't tell you much. There's no way for you to know who might be important to you later, so make sure you give everybody your attention and the most charming parts of your personality. If you act a little chilly to somebody you think is only a bean counter in the purchasing department, you might later find that bean counter putting your request for a new Macintosh on the bottom of the pile. That's what happened to a grad who came to work for a manager I talked to in the aerospace industry. His new hire had trouble getting stuff he ordered:

> He would expect that just because it was their job they would go ahead and do it and that they'd have

> the same sense of urgency that he had. What it really takes is nagging, following up, and expecting people to *not* do what they promised they would do. I think tact is a big part of it—learning how to talk to someone and not call up and say, "Aren't you being a little lazy about this?" and instead say, "Have you had a chance to do that five-minute task I put on your desk six weeks ago?"

That last line might not seem tactful, but you can pull it off without sounding hostile if you've already got a relationship going. You're pressing, but it's friendly.

In his company, which is huge, you can't get anything done without having good contacts in other departments. "You've got to develop a rapport with an individual in every place you have to deal with, every function you've got to work through."

Try to have at least a "Hi, there" acquaintance with everyone. Here are some of the people you might be tempted to blow off and why you're nuts if you do:

**Folks in Personnel** In some companies you'll pick up the distinct impression that a lot of people around you—even your boss and the other managers—think the people in the personnel department (the term human resources seems to be more p.c. these days) are a bunch of dweebs. That's because when a manager wants to hire, fire, or promote somebody, she's got to wade through an ocean of niggling rules that the personnel people enforce. This annoys managers. Half the time, though, this stuff isn't made up by the personnel staff—it's the law, as in you can't fire somebody over forty just because they're over forty. Managers don't like these rules. They like to do what they want. So they slide and skate around, trying to do what they want anyway and fighting with human resources along the way.

A manager will also often think that the people in personnel don't know anything about her department and that having them screen applicants is just a waste of time. What managers fail to realize is that the people department knows people. They usually have good bullshit detectors and can keep total phonies from getting in the door.

There are good reasons why you should *not* pick up a bad attitude about personnel from people around you. Remember that it's the personnel department that manages many of the company's perks and policies. Let's say at your company a certain kind of time-off accrues every year but drops off your chart if you don't take it by December 31. And you forget to take it. If you've got a friend in personnel, and you beg, he might put the hours back on for you.

When it's time to hand out raises, managers will often have to listen to the personnel folks to conform to guidelines, like merit pool rules and such (we'll get to that later). A personnel officer on your side can work wonders. Or let's say your boss turns out to be a weirdo and asks you to do the wild thing. It'll be a lot easier to bust him if you already feel comfortable talking to somebody in personnel. And, when *you* become a manager, and you have to deal with all the rules about hiring, firing, and promoting your staff, guess what?

**Secretaries** Secretaries know what goes on. They make the appointments, so they know who's meeting with whom, both inside and outside the company. They protect their bosses, so they know who the boss is trying to avoid, and why. They type up reports, so they know what projects are hot. Their bosses tell them their woes, so they know what mood the boss is in.

And that's just the direct info they have access to. Because they deal with so many people, they get the company buzz, and they usually get it first. There are times when just a shred of this information can save your hiney.

Remember that secretaries have been irked about the way they've been treated for about a century—and rightfully so—ever since the days when all companies were run by Big White Daddies and secretaries were "the girls." If you're patronizing or condescending or try to kiss up too much, a secretary will cut you off. And rightfully so. So just be real.

**Other People's Bosses** There are a lot of times in business when you might be working for someone other than your boss, so it's a good idea to get to know other managers ahead of time. Farther on down the line, you might find that you're contributing work to a project that is under their control. Or you might be loaned by your boss to a team supervised by someone else. Or there might be an organizational shakeup and, bam, you report to Carl Dimly instead of Susan B. Light. If Dimly already knows you to be upstanding and true, it'll be easier to work for him.

One way to learn about other bosses in your company is by the way their staff acts. If Jan can never give you an answer on anything without checking upstairs, you can bet her boss is a control freak. That's good to know if you ever have to work with him.

Another way is to just talk to them. There's no law that says you can't.

Everybody, from the folks in the mail room to the janitor, has info you can use. If you're too busy to care and act like they're androids who should do your bidding and then quietly go away, then you're just being stupid and deserve what you get.

## How to Get to Know 'Em

Back to making the introduction rounds on that first day. Right after introductions, you should try to get a little more info from whoever's introducing you—probably your boss. Ask questions like, "So Joe does the marketing. Is he also in charge of advertising, or is that someone else?" You can get all kinds of stories this way. Your boss might give you a knowing grin and say, "Well, Joe *used* to be in charge of advertising."

Even if your boss says nothing more, you've got a tip about something that happened with Joe.

Then talk to your coworkers. You might say, "I just met Joe in Marketing. So I hear he used to oversee advertising, too?" You might get a little more of the story. Before you know it, you're learning a lot about who does what and who *used* to do what, which will tell you a lot about the people and the way the company uses them. If you've got an organizational chart, check out where everybody you just met is on it. (More about the hierarchy later.)

During the following weeks you'll start going eyeball-to-eyeball (or E-mail to E-mail) with these folks; that's when you really start to check each other out. Entire books have been written about how this game is played, but it all boils down to two basic techniques: listening and observing.

**Listening** Make sure you listen more than you talk. Here's why: You get more info. You appear smart, like you're pondering what was just said. You're less likely to say something stupid. You get respect from who you're listening to because, well, you're *really listening*. "I ain't never learned nothin' by talkin'," said Lyndon Johnson. Ain't it the truth.

Listening isn't as easy as it sounds. You listened a lot in college, but you also learned not to listen. Since it was impossible to absorb every bit of wisdom that spewed forth from your professors' mouths, you learned to tune out. Now it's time to learn how to tune in again.

Here's how you *really* listen. Now pay attention:

• Focus • A visual word, but that describes it: zero in on the person you're listening to and what they're saying. Don't think that just because you heard what somebody said, and can even run it back to them word for word, that you got the point. You're being like the kid who says, "I heard you. You said my pants are on fire."

Research on listening shows that it takes a few seconds of real time to switch on your focus. If you pay attention, you can sense when you're rearranging the old synapses. Focusing is something you feel. It's like standing in one place while other ideas tug at you.

By the way, if you can't really focus, don't try to fake it. You might be able to fool game show hosts and some species of small dogs by faking the tips below, but your charade won't work on normal humans. People have a sixth sense about whether they're being listened to or not.

• SEND "I'M PAYING ATTENTION" SIGNALS • When somebody's talking, he's watching you make physical signals since you aren't making verbal ones. Every signal you give has an effect on what you're getting from him. Look at him on eye level (sit down if he's sitting), lean forward a little, stay at an appropriate distance, and keep your eyes on him with only occasional breaks. Act relaxed, not like you can't wait to talk about experiences that *you* had for *yourself*.

• DON'T SEND "I GOTTA GO" SIGNALS • If you're looking around the room like, "I wonder if there's a secret escape hatch behind that credenza," your talker is going to shut up. Ditto for wiggling—actually, for any physical movement that doesn't relate to the conversation. Communication expert Robert Bolton says this in his book *People Skills* (Touchstone):

"The good listener moves his body in response to the speaker. Ineffective listeners move their bodies in response to stimuli that are unrelated to the talker. Their distraction is demonstrated by their body language: fiddling with pencils or keys, jingling money, fidgeting nervously, drumming fingers, cracking knuckles, frequently shifting weight or crossing and uncrossing the legs, swinging a crossed leg up and down, and other nervous mannerisms."

So *sit still,* already.

• SHUT UP • Just don't talk. That means get out of the speaker's way so she can collect her thoughts. If you ask too many questions you'll be going down your road, not hers. If you have to ask a question to get things going, make it general. Don't say, "I get it. So then he won the client back but blew the account after all, right?" Just say, "So then what happened?"

Shutting up can be the *most* effective way to get information from someone. If there's a pause in the conversation, try letting it hang there. Pros have found out that that's when you get all kinds of juicy stuff. One worker I met has watched her CEO use this technique:

"The head of our company is a very thoughtful person. People say something during a meeting and he doesn't respond immediately. He thinks. And people shoot themselves with him by trying to fill in that gap. And they dig themselves into deeper and deeper holes. And he starts enjoying it."

So give it a rest and see what happens.

• HEAR WHAT'S UNDERNEATH • Why is the speaker saying what she's saying? What's motivating her to say it in this particular way at this particular time? Shrinks have a field day with this stuff, of course, and not without good reason. Psychiatrist Eric Berne thinks people have a script for themselves that they follow and that this is revealed in the way they talk. He described it in *What Do You Say After You Say Hello?* (Bantam):

"The first thing to be decided about a script is whether it is a winning one or a losing one. This can often be discovered very quickly by listening to the person talk. A winner says things like: 'I made a mistake,

> but it won't happen again,' or 'Now I know the right way to do it.' A loser says 'If only . . .' 'I should've . . .' and 'Yes, but . . .' There are also near misses, nonwinners whose scripts require them to work very hard, not for the purpose of winning, but just to stay even. These are 'at leasters,' people who say 'Well, at least I didn't . . .' or 'At least I have this much to be thankful for.' Nonwinners make excellent members, employees, and serfs, since they are loyal, hard-working, and grateful and not inclined to cause trouble. Socially, they are pleasant people, and in the community, admirable. Winners make trouble for the rest of the world only indirectly, when they are fighting among themselves and involve innocent bystanders, sometimes by the millions. Losers cause the most grief to themselves and others. Even if they come out on top they are still losers and drag other people down with them when the payoff comes."

I don't have a whole system worked out like Eric, but I have noticed a few patterns, one of which is defined by what I call Soden's Postulate. It states that "When someone offers a disclaimer at the beginning of a sentence, it means they're trying to hide what they really think, which is what they're disclaiming." Here's an example. When someone says "Now, I'm not saying he's a liar, but . . ." what they mean is "I think he's a liar. In fact it's the first thing I thought, but I don't want you to think I think that."

Listen not only for this kind of unconscious stuff but also for any spin your speaker is consciously trying to put on his talk. If he's mentioned several times that he's the one in charge of the rubber bands, maybe it's because he's afraid you've been hired as the new rubber band whiz. This tells you he's not very secure in his duties and that perhaps rubber band whizdom is up for grabs.

• Be aware of the male/female thing • No, not flirting. I'm talking about different communication patterns. In her book *You Just Don't Understand* (William Morrow), linguist Deborah Tannen explains the differences:

"Since women seek to build rapport, they are inclined to play down their expertise rather than display it. Since men value the position of center stage and the feeling of knowing more, they seek opportunities to gather and disseminate factual information."

This means that if you're listening to a member of the opposite sex, you might not be hearing what they're trying to tell you. If you're a man, and a woman coworker is telling you all about your boss's problems with his teenage son and you're thinking, "What does this have to do with work?"—you're not getting it. She's letting you know what kind of pressure he's under, and that has a lot to do with how he'll behave in the office. And if you're a woman and you're listening to a man, and he's droning on in boring detail about some marketing campaign, realize that it's something he's proud to know about and thinks knowing about it makes him important. Boring as it is, maybe it *is* important.

**Observing** We'll start with clothes. Do I really have to tell you that what people wear says a lot about them? I didn't think so. The working world, though, has its own language. Suits may all look the same to you, but if you want to learn to read execs you've got to apply the same discerning eye you use to spot phony Doc Martens.

The main thing bizpeople worry about is "what's appropriate." That is, nothing should be too odd. At the same time, they want to show that they have a superior sense of style. This shows off their knowledge of culture, their attention to detail, and their judgment, all of which are qualities used in the actual business of business.

Although you'll develop your own system, try this for starters. People can be placed into four different groups by the way they dress:

• CLUELESS AND DON'T CARE • Some of these people don't understand how *anyone* could be *so shallow* as to judge somebody else by their clothing. *They* will do nothing of the kind and refuse to dress to impress. Others just don't get it at all. "Whuduhya mean? I always wear white socks."

It's a good bet that the clueless crowd can't understand anybody else's value system, whether it has to do with clothing or putting together a presentation to the client. Some of these folks can only deal with quantifiable things, which is why computer nerds and number crunchers are often in this group.

• GOT A CLUE, BUT THAT'S ALL • They read a book, or heard a lecture, or somebody told them about the basics of business wear. They went right out and bought the safest, most boring clothing possible. The men wear dark suits and striped ties *every single day.* The women wear dark suits and white blouses *every single day.* The clothing is often cheap. These people like rules and don't have the imagination to move much beyond them.

• HAD A CLUE IN 1978 • These folks realize that you have to show some style but their style sense is a little, ah, twisted. For some, their fashion sense stopped a couple of decades ago. For others, they bring the wrong influence into the office. One of these guys will wear a suit, all right, but it'll look like something out of *Eraserhead.* They display the same exquisite judgment in the middle of a meeting, suggesting that the president make the next press conference a "photo opportunity" by wrestling down prices with Hulk Hogan.

• CLUED IN • Those who get it. They always look right, never lame, never unbusinesslike and somehow cool at the same time. It's a mystery how they do it. Often people like this can work the same kind of voodoo on their work projects—but not always.

I can't give you specifics about what kind of clothing is the power look for your office. Beware of any book that tries. The look is different depending on about a million factors: where you live (the East Coast, West Coast thing), the field you're in (finance or making infomercials), the department you're in (sales or computer programming), etc. The categories above work, but only if you know the particulars. Somebody in the advertising department of your company who wears jeans, for example, may have more power than an office manager who wears a suit every day.

When you're studying your coworkers, don't stop at their clothes. Here are some other things to take note of:

• OFFICES • Like clothes, offices speak volumes. Samantha covers her wall with degrees and honors—every certificate from every seminar she ever took. She's obviously somebody who believes in the Official Validation of Knowledge. If you need to convince her of something, make sure you get your info from somebody with impressive credentials in the field.

Barry's got pictures of himself with his family, his fishing buddies, the little league he coaches. He's a guy who values ties between people. How well you work with him will depend on how much he feels you're a part of his network.

Bill's office is blank. Zippo on the walls, nothing on the desk but paper. He's probably a real no-nonsense guy, someone who feels guilty if he chats too much on company time. To work with Bill, stick to business.

Most people don't hide who they are, especially in their offices. It's their personal space; it says personal stuff about them, so study it closely.

• NONWORK TIME • Say you go out to lunch with your coworkers. Phil orders the waitress around like he's Prince Charles. Sherry follows a totally weird diet, is very inflexible about it, and indulges her strong urge to tell you all about why it's the superior way to eat. She probably knows the superior way for everyone to do their job, too.

Anytime you're with coworkers in a nonwork situation—carpooling to work, chatting in the hall, going to the company picnic—check out their behavior and then imagine that kind of behavior in a work situation. You'll learn a lot.

## How to Get Known

While you're checking out everyone else, they'll be checking you out. The first thing you should do to prepare for this is to reread all the advice I just gave you about reading people and reverse the situation. For example, I suggested you ask people leading questions like, "Is Joe in charge of advertising?" Realize that people are going to be asking you these kind of questions, too. If they know you're fresh out of college (as if they can't smell it on you) they'll ask where you went, what you majored in, etc. Have some brilliant comments worked out so you can say more than just the facts. If you did an internship, tell them about it, and what you learned there.

They'll be listening to you just like I told you to listen to them. They'll be trying to listen to what's underneath, and they've got the advantage because they're in a comfortable space while you're probably nervous. So think about what you're sounding like. A neophyte who's pretending she knows more than she does? A smart ass who sounds like he thinks work is a joke? A kiss-ass who can't be trusted? They'll be listening *close,* my friend.

They'll be looking at your clothes, too, so go over that list and try to hit the right style. For starters, it's much better to lean toward the safe and boring. You can push the envelope later.

On another level, they'll be using their own private system to figure you out, and I can't tell you what that is. It might be from that smash business best-seller *How to Swim With Naked Sharks Who Sell Shirts* or from some seminar they took or from the *Tibetan Book of the Dead.*

Don't worry too much about what their system is; just be aware of the stuff you could be doing that would make them believe something about you. You might notice that they're always trying to have meetings in their office instead of yours. It's their little power play. Even if you think the whole idea is stupid, you might want to figure out a way to get them to your office. If you do it, they'll respect you, even though you think the whole game is a goof.

When you get down to the work, there are two common ways people will mess with you as a sort of test. The first is to see how far they can push you when they need something. The second is to see if they can blow you off when you need something.

**How Far Can They Push You?** Most of the time when somebody asks you to do something, it's just part of the job. But sometimes it's a dominance thing. Whoever's asking is thinking (maybe not even consciously), "Can I order this kid around, even though I'm not his boss? Let's see."

In one job I had, I was in charge of getting the company's brochures produced. People from different departments would come with requests and I'd have to fit their project into a schedule. After I'd been there only a week or two, this guy comes storming into my cubicle and says, "I need a flyer done today. It'll only take you a minute." He was right that it wouldn't take long to do the work, but I wasn't going to drop everything I was doing just because he said so. I sensed I was being tested. I told him I'd work it into the schedule and get back to him about when it could be done. He didn't like it, but he went away.

The next morning I delivered the flyer to him, all finished. I told him I'd made a special effort to get it out because I knew he needed it right away. By not giving him the flyer when he asked for it, I established that my time was under my control, not his. By giving him the completed brochure when he only expected to be given a date when it would be done, I let him know that I was willing to listen to what he needed and to try to help him out. To me, all this posturing was stupid, but that's how he played the game, so I played along. And it worked. After that, he regarded me as an equal. I saw him try to bully other new people; if he succeeded, he treated them like servants from then on.

**How Far Will You Push Them?** When you're new and you ask somebody to do something for you, that's also a test. A lot of times people won't do what you ask not because they're trying to stiff you but just because somebody more important is ahead of you. We're not talking about importance in terms of your title or position. We're talking about clout. That comes from a lot of things like who you know, what you know, and how you're perceived. When you start, none of this is going for you. All you have is your ability to be persistent. If it's somebody's job to get pencils and you ask them for a pencil, then damn it, keep after them until they give you one.

This can be a hard lesson to learn. You need to have a variety of nudges. Here are a few:

- JUST BUG 'EM • No secret here; just call them every day and ask them if the job is done yet. At first you'll feel like a giant pain doing this, but you should remember one thing: they're not doing you a favor, they're just doing their job. A lot of times when you call, you'll find that the person on the other end feels a lot more guilty about falling behind than you do about calling.

• LET THEM KNOW WHAT WON'T HAPPEN IF THEY DON'T DELIVER • Where I worked before, Jim was president. So if you said, "I need this for a project I'm working on for Jim," magical things would happen. Nobody wanted to disappoint the president.

If you can't drop a name, try to get your target to share in feeling responsible for what could go wrong if the project isn't completed. Don't say, "My boss'll kill me if this isn't done Monday." Sam in Research is just going to think, "Well, that's your problem, buddy." Instead, put it in terms of the company. Think of how your work will contribute to some larger project, preferably one Sam is worried about. Then say, "If I don't get those stats, we might just have to deliver the report to the client a week late."

• TELL YOUR BOSS • Don't whine and don't crucify the guy. Play it very low-key. Just say, "I was going to have that report to you on Monday, but Sam in Research seems to be having a little *trouble* with the stats."

• PUT IT IN WRITING • When all else fails, write a memo to Sam repeating what you said verbally: that unless he gets moving the whole project will be late. Now, here's the important part: *send copies of the memo to your boss and Sam's boss.* Sending the memo only to Sam probably won't do any more good than talking to him did. It's getting the higher-ups involved that will make him move. Be careful, though: keep your wording extra low-key. Don't place blame. (More info on how to use memos is in *Trekking the Paper Trail,* Chapter 6.)

Two last things about getting known:

• START STRONG • Put everything you've got into your first few weeks. Be as impressive as you can stand to be without going insane. Later, when you start to slack off, or if you really screw something up, people will think it's "out of character" and will assume that you'll get back to your normal sterling self. They'll *help* you get back, if you need it. But if you start off as a flake, you'll be branded a flake even if you get better. That's just the way it works.

• BE LIKABLE • Above all else, try to be somebody that people like. Some bizfolks make a huge mistake because they think it doesn't matter if people like them "as long as they *respect* me." Wrong, wrong, wrong. Here's what Roger Ailes (adviser to U.S. presidents and general p.r. guru) says:

"If you could master one element of personal communications that is more powerful than anything we've discussed, it is the quality of being likable. I call it the magic bullet, because if your audience likes you, they'll forgive just about everything else you do wrong. If they don't like you, you can hit every rule right on target and it doesn't matter."

## That Schmoozemeister Feeling

All this schmoozing seems sort of artificial, doesn't it? You're probably ready to bag the whole thing and sit in your cubicle with your Walkman cranked up to top volume. You can do that. Or you can just use some of my suggestions and forget the rest if they really seem sleazy to you.

There's only one point to all of this, and that is that you should choose the method you're comfortable with. What you're trying to do is to simply figure out who you can rely on: who's going to help you and who won't. Once you find that out, you're done. Don't be constantly glad-handing and watching your back. It's a distraction. Take Tom Harrison's advice: "Pick the people you're going to trust, and trust 'em."

## Your E-Z Guide to Office Politics

What's that you say? *You'd* never stoop to the backstabbing, butt-kissing, humiliating, unethical, and generally cheesy behavior that goes on in offices across America? Good. You just made your first political move.

You cannot escape politics unless you're totally alone or dead. Politics is just the word that describes how we deal with each other to get what we want. You *do* want things, don't you?

By saying you want to avoid politics, you mean you want to avoid compromising your beliefs. That's good—it gives you the foundation to know what it is you want to get.

The hard part of office politics is that they're probably a lot more complicated than what you're used to. In the typical company there are a lot of players at all different power levels, each trying to achieve separate goals.

**The Four Harsh Realities of Planet Bizness** But let's back up a minute and lay the groundwork. There are certain givens in the business world that are just part of the landscape. They're so deeply imbedded in the way our economic system works that they can't be changed without reforming society. Here are the Four Harsh Realities that form the bedrock of office politics:

- THE CUSTOMER IS ALWAYS RIGHT • The customer might be the client, the retailer, the buyer, or the government that funds the project: whoever's paying the bills, that's the customer.

• COMPANIES MUST MAKE MONEY • That's what companies do. Even nonprofit companies must make enough money to pay their staff, or they're outta there.

• COMPANIES MUST EXPLOIT HUMAN TALENT, SKILL, AND LABOR TO MAKE MONEY • It would be nice if we could all go on vacation and let RoboManagers take over, but it ain't gonna happen.

• COMPANIES ARE ORGANIZED INTO HIERARCHIES • There's a lot of talk about teamwork and empowering every employee to make decisions and take responsibility. But the truth is, essentially all companies are pyramid shaped and based on obedience.

Another way to look at these realities is like this:

- The customers control the money.
- The money controls the company.
- The company controls the people.
- The people control each other.

So where do politics come in? As I said, we use politics to get what we want; the ability to get what we want is called power.

**The Three Commandments of Bright Ideas** What people in business really fight for is power, but they argue about it in terms of what the company wants, which is defined by the Harsh Realities above. People who are successful in office politics obey the Three Commandments of Bright Ideas:

• Thou shalt sell ideas in terms of the Four Harsh Realities better than thou's rivals • The biggest mistake most people make in trying to sell their ideas is that they sell them in terms of *their* wish list, not the company's. "I *deserve* to be promoted to Regional Director of Wingnut Production! After all, I've spent two years winging it out in the field!"

• Thou shalt sell ideas that will increase thee's power and thy company's power • It's sort of like holding yourself for ransom. "If you take my idea, you'll have to take the kid, too."

• Thou shalt sell ideas as a bandwagon others can jump on to increase their own power • "You know, Dave, they really should have made you Regional Wingnut Director. What if we put together our own team and sold them on the idea of a new division? I could be Manager of Marketing, and you could be Director. Then we'd . . ."

Those are the basics. Let's see how this works out in the real world.

One manager I talked to, whom we'll call Susan, worked in the government relations department of a large company. The company often built new facilities that required city approval. The company had a real estate department to do just that. In her dealings with the city government, however, Susan found out that the real estate folks were blowing it left and right. They weren't paying attention to changing city regulations, so they were missing opportunities. Since Susan knew how to jump through the city hoops, she knew she'd be able to save the company time and money.

Susan could have simply gone to the real estate department and offered her expertise on an ongoing basis to help them improve their track record. That would have helped the company but wouldn't have helped her politically. Instead, she observed the Three Commandments:

**She Sold in Terms of the Four Harsh Realities** She explained to her boss how the real estate department was screwing up and how her plan would help the company. In this case, she sold her idea on three of the four forces. She skipped number one (*The customer is always right*)—although it's true that building new facilities would please customers, that was already a given, and not part of her idea. Using number two—*Companies must make money*—she showed how the company could save money (which is almost as good as making it) by understanding the city approval system. She appealed to number three—*Companies must exploit human talent*—noting how the company could better exploit her talents and the talents of the folks in the real estate department by combining their actions. And she appealed to number four—*Companies are organized into hierarchies*—by implying that in this case the hierarchy had broken down; the man in charge of the real estate department was not controlling his workers as well as he should have been.

**She Sold an Idea That Would Increase Her Power As Well As the Company's** Susan suggested she be put in charge of the team taking new facilities through city approval. Her argument was that because city approval was turning out to be the determining factor in the price of new facilities and her expertise was in government relations, then she should head the team. After the deal was struck and commitments made all around, then she could turn the real estate staff loose to attend to the pesky details.

**She Sold an Idea That Would Increase the Power of Those Who Would Support Her** In this case, Susan offered her idea as a bandwagon for her boss. If her power increased, that enlarged the scope and power of his department. Although they both knew it was a direct challenge to the real estate department's authority, they believed the potential reward was worth it.

Since neither Susan nor her boss could directly ask for control, the maneuvering took place in meetings where Susan subtly brought out the mistakes and misunderstandings the real estate department had made. She would describe what should have been done and why, thus displaying her expertise for all to see. Needless to say, the real estate folks were not happy. As Susan tells it, "I was not well-liked on certain floors of the building."

Eventually enough evidence was brought to light that Susan's boss could go to the head of the real estate department and offer the "help" of his staff member, proposing that she lead the team. The man agreed; he was close to retirement and was happy to relinquish control. In another company, the person in that position might have fought bitterly.

The plan worked: Susan was given more power, the company got a better deal, and Susan's boss expanded his empire.

## What to Know Before Making Your First Ruthless Power Grab

Before you jump into the political pit, check the big picture through the lens of the Four Harsh Realities. Then plan your pitch using the Three Commandments for Bright Ideas. Finally, use this list o' tips to make your day-to-day moves:

**To Get Supporters, Give As Well As Receive** At the same time you're trying to move your plans along, others are trying to move theirs. Don't approach them with the idea that they're going to drop what they're doing just so they can catapult you to the top. Give them your attention. Listen closely to what they have to say. (See the section on listening, above.) They won't help you unless they know you'll help them. Another reason to listen is a very simple one: their idea may be better than yours. They might have a bandwagon you can ride, one that will get you farther with less risk.

**Sell People One by One** Don't pitch your idea to a room full of people. The dynamics will be out of your control. Go to your potential supporters one at a time so you can judge their response, answer their questions, cater to their needs. Do this to a number of people. Once you have them on your side, then you can call a meeting or send out a plan.

**Don't Hesitate to Ask for Help** When people do you a favor, they are as bound to you as if you had done a favor for them. This is the technique politicians use over and over again to reinforce their networks. The reason it works is that when someone does you a favor they are investing in you. They will continue to help you to ensure that their investment pays off.

**Pick Your Side and Stay on It** Political moves only work if you can take a head count to see whom you can depend on for support. Other people will want to count on you just as you want to count on them. Don't try to stay neutral and make all sides happy. You can do that, but your opinion will be seen as inconsequential. And since you're going to stick with a side, take time to make sure you've got the right one to begin with.

**Don't Avoid Your Enemies** Go out of your way to talk to the jerks who oppose you—and keep the talk friendly. Why? First, to show you're not afraid of them. Second, it makes it harder for them to make you the bad guy. If they never see you, it's so much easier for them to hang all their hostilities on you, both professional and personal. Third, you'll learn more about their position, the better to ridicule it.

If you're in a position to lead a team, *ask an enemy to join you.* If you leave her out, you're giving her a motive to dump on your team's work. If she's part of the process (which you are leading, and so can help shape) you're giving her a reason to make the team a success. And to everyone else you'll be seen as magnanimous.

**Set Your Goals Low and Your Sights High** People in business depend on each other. You can't do much alone, and that's different than it was in college. When you say you'll do something, you've got to come through, so it's crucial that you give yourself easy targets. When you tell someone how long it will take you to do something, tell them it will take twice as long as you really think it will. When someone asks you how much a project will cost, tell them twice as much as you think. Then go ahead and try to do the job in half the time with half the budget. This accomplishes two things.

First, when you come in ahead of time and under budget consistently, you'll get a reputation as someone who can make things happen. Taken to the extreme, this trick is called *low-balling*—something politicians do all the time. They tell the press how hard it will be to beat their opponent. When they do, it's a David and Goliath story. You don't have to take it that far, but the effect is similar. Second, there will be times when you'll need to use that extra cushion, and then some, especially when you're new and you're not aware of everything that can go wrong.

I know, I know, you probably can't double your estimates. I just said that for effect. Increase them as much as you can, though—no kidding.

At first you may feel guilty about bumping up your estimates. Don't. All smart managers do it. You *should* feel guilty, though, if you slack off in trying to come in under your projections. If you make a habit of that, you'll find yourself blowing deadlines, budgets, and your rep.

**When You Screw Up, Be the First to Tell About It** Tell your boss, and don't be afraid to tell other people too. That way you control the time and place of the news getting around. If you don't tell your boss first, and she finds out later, woe is you. Telling her ahead of time should at least impress her that you're not trying to hide anything.

**Position Yourself** In marketing, positioning means finding a niche for a product that isn't occupied already. Is Jive Cola going to be the gourmet soda of the decade, made from rare cola berries handpicked by specially trained farmers? Or is it going to be the bargain of the nineties? Is it the old classic, the way soda should be made, or the brand-new innovation? Like it or not, your coworkers will try to tag you the same way a product is tagged. You can either make a conscious effort to influence their perception or risk that they'll do the obvious, which is to dump you into a pre-existing stereotype. "Jason? Oh, he's just another one of those up-tight guys in accounting."

When I got a job as publication designer, I wore a suit to work. Nobody had seen a designer do that. After all, as an artsy person, the designer had the privilege of wearing jeans. By wearing a suit I threw off the easy perception that I was a flaky artist. Soon the people in charge of funding campaigns were letting me write their appeals as well as design them. In another job, although I wore a suit, my office was artsy and my style of working casual and brainstormy. In other words, I positioned myself as the slightly eccentric but creative executive.

If you make yourself difficult to categorize, people will pay more attention to your individual characteristics. The trick is to fit in and stand out at the same time.

**Make 'Em Laugh** What? What's this tip on humor doing in the political section of this book? Because it's damn important, that's why, and it's something a lot of grim-faced graduates forget when they walk through the doors of Spudlicker Potato Products, Inc. Nothing gives you away as not being in control faster than being real, real serious. If you're not relaxed enough to crack a joke, or at least a smile, then others will spot you as someone easy to rattle. When that happens, bingo, you're on the defensive. Here's what Mark McCormack says about humor in *What They Don't Teach You at Harvard Business School*:

> Laughter is the most potent, constructive force for diffusing business tension, and you want to be the one who controls it. If you can point out what is humorous or absurd about a situation or confrontation and diffuse the tension by getting the other party to share your feeling, you will be guaranteed the upper hand. There are very few absolutes in business. This is one of them, and *I've never seen it fail.*

When you walk into a new situation, try to lighten things quickly with a mildly humorous comment. Don't start with an actual joke—that stops everyone in their tracks and forces them to be your audience. If you blow the joke you'll be in worse shape than before. Just say something a little witty. If nobody smiles, then you can quit.

Humor can be a shortcut to emotional connections because it binds people into "us" (We Who Have Laughed Together) and "them" (Everyone Else). If you make a reference to something, say in Pop culture for example, you can get a quick read on how aware your coworker is of what's going on. Their comeback can tell you more. To wit: you say, "Don't you think the prez and v.p. act like Ren and Stimpy—or is it just me?" to which your meetingmate replies, "Yeah, but I think Stimpy's got a few I.Q. points on the old guy."

Self-deprecating humor is always good, as long as you don't make it too pointed. Don't say things like, "I'm so low on the totem pole I'd have to be *promoted* to be the gofer, heh, heh!"

So, remember: Never, *never* laugh or tell amusing anecdotes in a business setting or you will get fired. (I make joke.)

## Stupid Political Tricks

If you think to succeed in office politics means being a lying hypocrite, think again. Snowing people and being two-faced are the marks of an amateur who has no political skills. Two examples follow for your amusement.

**Lying** Aside from the fact that it's obnoxious, lying is hard to keep track of—who you lied to, what you said to them—it's a pain. Once, in a meeting, I heard a manager rave on about how stupid it was that certain information was released to customers. Someone pointed out that *she* was the one who released it, in a memo. She denied ever sending out a memo like that. Someone then produced the memo—with her signature on it. She said *someone else* had written it and misrepresented what it was to get her to sign it. Her excuse was pathetic. Her political clout fell a couple of hundred points below zero.

**Hypocrisy** If you always say what people want to hear, no one will listen to you. And don't think you can get away with being two-faced just because you're talking to somebody outside your company. Once I was on a team that prepared an advertising campaign for a client. When she came, she picked one of our three layouts and praised it up and down. Anticipating that she was a hard sell, we even got her to sign an approval form. Everyone left happy—we thought. When she got back to her boss, we heard from another source that she had told him how incompetent we were and how the campaign was a waste of time. From that moment on, we took advantage of every opportunity to make her job miserable in any way we could.

## Yelling and Other Unpleasantness

In school, you probably didn't have anyone yell at you except the occasional coach. The disapproving lecture, the raised eyebrows, the stern grimace—you might have gotten any one of these from a prof at some point in your academic career. If you're lucky, that's all you'll have to deal with at work, too. If you're unlucky, you run into somebody who measures their power in decibels. It might be your boss, or it may be a coworker. I once had what I thought was a mild disagreement with a coworker in front of our boss. Bill smiled, and stated a different opinion. After our boss left, he calmly invited me into his office, where he shut the door and screamed at me at the top of his lungs for a full five minutes. "If you *EVER* contradict me in front of Marty again," he roared, "I will get you fired!" I cowered, and left. I also quit shortly after that, having no idea what to do.

Here's where relationships at work can get really confusing. I've already told you that your boss is not like one of your parents. Yet he may yell at you, which probably is like something your parents may have done. It's easy to want to revert to whatever your kid techniques were—bellowing back, going into a snit, or crying. Try not to do that. Try to stay focused on the work issues. Remember that if someone yells at you all the time, it's really their problem.

Chapter 3

# Clients and Other Money People

IF YOU'VE MADE IT THIS FAR AND DONE EXACTLY WHAT I TOLD YOU, YOU NOW HAVE YOUR BOSS SAYING STUFF LIKE, "GOOD JOB, TRAVIS," AND YOUR COWORKERS THINKING YOU'RE BOTH A NICE GUY AND A SLY DOG, TOO. DON'T KICK BACK YET, THOUGH. NOTICE THOSE NICE PEOPLE OUTSIDE THE COMPANY, THE ONES WHO BUY YOUR COMPANY'S PRODUCT OR SERVICE? THEY'RE CALLED CUSTOMERS OR CLIENTS.

And what about those smiley people who come by, offering to take people out to lunch? They're vendors. You might not have to deal with either of them—but then again, you might. And if you do, you've got to be smooth. Blow it, and you'll be living the "Night of the Unemployed."

Clients. Vendors. You. That's the basic division, although it's a little more complicated than that. By clients, I include customers, retailers (if your company is a manufacturer), patrons (if you work at a museum); in other words, the people who pay money to your company for what your company produces. For simplicity, I'll refer to them all as clients. If you work at a big company, there are people inside that you should also treat as clients if you don't want your butt thrown out the door. You might, for example, work in the research department, where your responsibility is to provide information (your product) to other staff members (your clients).

By the way, I should mention that there's one management fad (sometimes called the customer service model) that says that *everybody* in a company is in the customer service business. Managers, for example, serve their employees. So you are your boss's customer. Yeah, right. Another management idea floating about a billion light years above These United States.

When I refer to vendors, I mean anybody who supplies your company with what it needs to run—suppliers, manufacturers, consultants, lawyers, bookies (just kidding). You get the picture.

Beyond that, there are people who don't fall into such neat categories. If you work in government or a nonprofit company that gets public money, you might have funders. These aren't exactly like clients. In some cases, they might be more like bosses. Or you might work someplace that has donors, alumni, or students—people who shell out the bucks but aren't quite customers.

On the quasi-vendor side, your company may have particular people outside who provide services so essential that business would collapse without them. Counting Crows, for example, might be considered a supplier that contributes a bit to the health of Geffen Records.

For those of you who've been catching a few z's through the previous chapters, I'll repeat the basic axiom about business: business is about money. It's not about friendship, family, respect, or obligation, although all those things come into play because we're the warm and fuzzy ape. But when you start thinking about the relationships you have with clients and vendors, think money first. Think of the other stuff as an overlay.

So take a look at the money pipes. Money flows into your company from clients and out to vendors. In its most brutal form, then, clients are the boss of you and you are the boss of vendors.

But this simplistic view is just the tip of the Titanic, and it won't carry you very far if you're sinking and need them to toss you a float. The reason is simple. In the relationship described above, one group is at the mercy of another group. Not only is this bothersome to those who are being bossed (they have their pride, you know) but as you've probably noticed, all relationships turn out to be gummier than they first seem.

Anyway, below I try to lay out some of the ways you, clients, and vendors might do the dance. We begin with clients.

## First Impressions, or Maybe Mr. Jenkins Likes Nose Rings

If you think dressing a certain way for work is a pain but important, think of dressing for clients as the Spanish Inquisition. In other words, you've got to feel confident and focused to deal with clients. If you get rattled for any reason, you might clam up or yammer on, whatever your particular nervous tic is. And even if you make it through without saying anything stupid, you'll forget what they said to you because you were distracted.

You've got to feel like you look good, sound good, and smell good so you can forget about it and do business. Here's a story that Hillary tells that illustrates the point:

> I had to talk to a small department store to try to convince them to use some of our phone services.

> It was my first client visit, and I was very nervous about what to wear. Somehow I had forgotten my work shoes and I only had my ugly little driving shoes, and I had to go in with those. I had a suit on with a white blouse that I would ordinarily have worn a camisole under, but I couldn't find a camisole, so I decided to keep my suit jacket on and figured it'd be fine. I get to the meeting and I'm talking and I'm explaining what's going on and I look down and I notice my buttons are unbuttoned. That's my memory of the meeting. I don't know what anybody else remembers from the meeting.

The best way to feel confident with clients is to try to fit in with their idea of appropriate dress. That doesn't mean you should wear a surgical mask if you're meeting with doctors, but you can often tweak your appearance in the direction your client uses.

Ed Seider worked as someone who put together environmental clean-up systems for industry. His clients ran the gamut, from suited executives to engineers with pocket protectors to field workers in overalls. Here's what he says:

> People feel most comfortable when they perceive you as one of their own, and appearance has a lot to do with that. If you can mirror them and their corporate image, then you are miles ahead from the outset. If you walk in dressed in a three-piece suit with a bunch of nice jewelry on to a company that basically dresses in jeans and boots, you're going to lose their trust right off the bat. At the same time, if you walk in wearing jeans and boots to a company with starch-white button-downs, they're going to look at you like you don't know what you're talking about. They're thinking, "How can this guy be successful? He's in jeans." I would

> actually try to find out in advance, maybe from a receptionist or somebody else at the company I felt comfortable with, how people dressed at the company.

You probably won't be able to adjust your outfit for every client you see, but if you can do any adjustment, do it. You'll feel better.

So much for your form. As for content, it's obvious that you should be as prepared as possible for any question the client might ask. Bring notes, brochures, diagrams—anything your company has that might remotely relate to the client. Go over it ahead of time so you feel confident.

Practice three or four intelligent-sounding "I don't know" lines so you don't have to say something like "Gosh, they didn't tell me that." Lines like, "I don't have that information available right now, but I'll find out the answer and give you a call tomorrow," or "I'm glad you brought that up. Our Rocket Science division specializes in that and can give you all the details you need. I'll be glad to put you in touch with Ms. Oppenheimer. I'm sure she can answer all your questions." I know I don't need to tell you that the more prepared you are, the more confident you'll feel. So I'm not telling you. I'm telling the other guy reading this book.

## Journey to the Center of a Client's Brain

To understand clients, you simply have to keep two conflicting ideas in your head at the same time. On one hand, clients are just like you. You're a client every time you order a pizza, so you know what it feels like if you get pepperoni instead of pineapple or if the pizza gets delivered an hour after Madge and Stu left the party. Looking at it this way, clients just want a fair deal.

On the other hand, clients are not like you at all. They don't care if their demands cause your company to lose time, money, or other clients. And ultimately they don't care if you're sent to count the no-smoking signs in the lobby of the unemployment office. It's money, remember? Don't take it personally.

Think of your attitude as a spectrum, like this:

Client is reasonable like me . . .
Client is bugging me . . .
I wish this client would go pound sand

Always start on the left and move to the right in baby steps, and only when you've got hard evidence. And don't think that a pissed-off client means he's a jerk whom you can impale on the hood ornament of your car. He may have a good reason for being pissed. Even if he is a jerk and has a bad reason for being pissed, you shouldn't handle him the way you would normally handle a jerk. He's a client, remember?

But let's start with the basics. Remember the money pipe. Because money comes from clients and business is money, clients *are* your company. No clients, no money, no business. As plainly, ridiculously simplistic as this sounds, it's not that easy to remember every single day when you see your boss scraping and bowing to some blowhard client who's two scoops short of a banana split. Lupé, our friend the advertising exec, finds that new grads can barely stand the idea that they have to be extra careful every time they communicate with a client:

> A new grad might have to rewrite a letter to a client two or three times. College students typically write sort of flowery. They'll think, "Why do I have to show you my letter, why are you criticizing me, why are you doing this? I'm smart, I come from a big school, I don't need to take your criticism." But a client is worth a lot of money. We

> don't want to jeopardize that with a letter. Even one letter that makes somebody mad, or has the wrong tone can jeopardize the client relationship.

The right attitude doesn't come naturally—it's something you've got to learn. It's a strange combination of respect, candor, and, well, deceit.

**The Respect Part** That's real respect, not "Yes, sir, [*sotto voce*] you stupid dweeb." Don't think of it as respect for this or that particular individual; think of it as respect for clients in general. It's really easy to get in the habit of thinking that clients don't know what they're talking about, largely because they often don't. They don't know your business; they just know what they want. One might call up and say, "Yeah, hi, I've got this, uh, well it's a part you guys made, I think, uh, it's got, you know, a deal sticking off of the left-hand side, and then it curves down to this rubber, whaduya call it, gasket, I think . . ."

Now if you say, "Sir, our company makes three hundred and sixty-five parts for seven different models of vacuum cleaners," you're just being pissy and you know it. The guy on the phone is just trying to fix his vacuum cleaner. Give him a break.

If you breezed over the above, and it didn't stir your ruthless heart, try out this reason for respect: the client you treat well today could be one that gives you tons of business tomorrow. Gather 'round, and let me tell you my true tale:

> Once there was long-haired young man with little money who was helping his guitar-playing friend have a flyer printed. It was a small job, costing less than fifty dollars. The first printer to which the young man went took the lad's money and gave him an ill-looking flyer. "I'm sorry, sir," the young

> man said, "but this job is so lacking in quality it fails to meet even *my* modest standards." The printer replied, "Then take your money back and be off with you!" Soon the boy was at the door of a second printer. "Please, sir," he said, "Would it be possible for you to provide the care I require for my humble handbill?" The kindly printer replied, "Why, of course." And although the profit was meager, this printer was generous with his time and produced a fine broadside. And it came to pass that six months later the young man had a new job as one who controlled the printing budget at a prominent college. The young man returned to the kindly printer many times, and for seven years gave him thousands and thousands of dollars worth of business.

**The Deceit and Candor Parts** Those of you who habitually leaf through these pages to see how long the sections are will have noticed that this section on deceit and candor is a tad longer than the one above on respect. That's because I know that respect comes naturally to all you gentle souls. I'm going to have to spend some time teaching you how to deftly blend deceit and candor; how to swirl together the white lie and the half-truth.

But why deceive? Because, as you know, your company is One Big Happy Family. Do Big Happy Family members go blabbing about how their brothers and sisters scratch their butts when they watch TV? Of course not. When asked about it, they fib. One of your jobs is to hide your company's butt-scratching.

It's usually not hard to remember to keep your mouth shut when you first start dealing with a client. That's a natural tendency with any new person you meet. But later, as you get to know and like them, you'll feel yourself wanting to come clean, perhaps, about some little thing the company did that might not have been in the client's best interest. Or you might want to give them that little extra info that can make their life easier. That's what happened to a guy I'll call Dave when he was working on Wall Street right out of grad school:

> This client was a portfolio manager and wanted an update on a company that we had underwritten a security offering for, one he had invested in. And I gave him more detail than I should have. It didn't affect the market, the company, or his investment in it, but it was something that should not have been passed on. I passed this information on, without even knowing it, really.

Dave got the word from his boss that this release of pure candor was too powerful, even though there was no harm done. The episode colored his boss's view so much that Dave thinks it stopped him from rising further in the company. It all worked out, though, because Dave blew off Wall Street and is now happily working for another company. But looking back, he realized just how delicate the candor/deceit mixture was, and that nobody had given him the recipe:

> I don't know where the blame really falls in that situation; if it was on the company for not spelling out where that boundary was, if it was on me for not knowing where the boundary was, or if it was on my boss for knowing I was not the one who should have been talking to the client. You can point a lot of fingers, but it comes down to a person going into a company and having to decide what should or shouldn't be done without the benefit of experience with that particular company. You should clarify things that you are uncertain about with your boss or even your coworkers.

The rule, then, is don't tell more about anything, even if it seems harmless, even if you've known the client for months and you're sure she wouldn't tell a soul.

At the same time, if you don't seem candid with your client, she'll assume you're hiding something and that it must be bad. For your clients to have trust in you, you've got to give them information. So you've got to seem wonderfully candid and truthful and informative and yet conceal certain things.

Seem impossible? Well, it's one of those "challenges" they talk about in the bizworld. It's often referred to as "thinking on your feet" as in "keep them on the floor so they're not suddenly tickling your tonsils."

## The Shell Game, or, When the Mouth Is Quicker Than the Ear

To help you assess what you should and shouldn't be telling, try this: First think of the information you have not as truth and lies but as information with three different degrees of sensitivity:

• STUFF I WILL TELL COMPLETELY WITHOUT HESITATION BECAUSE IT'S PART OF THE JOB •

• STUFF A CLIENT HAS TO PRESS ME TO GET • When I give it, the client will think of it as a favor or as something I reveal reluctantly.

• STUFF I WILL NOT TELL, EVEN IF THEY PUT ME IN A SMALL ROOM WITH BAD COFFEE AND THE MUZAK VERSION OF "RAINDROPS KEEP FALLING ON MY HEAD" •

Now, in a dramatic use of metaphor, I suggest you imagine that you've set up a small white magician's table with three shells on it. Under the three shells are the three kinds of info.

Across from you sits the client, wondering which shell has what he wants underneath.

You, of course, always start by uncovering Shell Number 1, the information you want to give. A well-behaved client will accept it, and you can have a nice chat. No prestidigitation necessary.

But this often isn't the scenario. Instead, you'll get a client who'll keep saying, "Oh, yeah? Well what's under that shell over there?" That's when you become Manipulo the Magnificent. Your job is to keep shifting and rearranging the shells so that the client always picks the one with the information you want to give and never picks the one with the deep dark secrets.

Let's take a real life example so you can get an idea of how this works. Here's the setup. Let's say a Mr. Denzkogger is calling trying to find out why an order is late. During his call you find the order sitting on the floor by the trash can when you thought you'd turned it in weeks ago. The reason it even fell off your desk in the first place is that your company has a rule that says orders must be submitted no more than three weeks before the needed delivery date. This rule bugs the hell out of everybody, because people have to keep the orders in their offices for weeks, where they're likely to get lost, just as Mr. Denzkogger's did.

Think about all the information you have about this situation, divide it up, and put it under the shells. Here, I'll do it for you:

> **Shell Number 1: Info I will freely give:** When the order was placed. Any information on the order. The usual time the company takes to process an order. What the company usually does to correct a late delivery.
>
> **Shell Number 2: Info I'd rather not give but will if I have to:** That you lost the order and forgot to turn it in. (You may think you're trying to

keep this from Mr. Denzkogger just because you're a skin-saving weasel, but there's more to it than that. If you look bad, your company looks bad.) That you will, if you have to, beg Jerry in Shipping to get the shipment delivered, and fast. (You're probably going to do this anyway, but you'd rather not have to admit this to Mr. Denzkogger.)

**Shell Number 3: Information I won't give:** That the company's ordering system sucks and that this happens all the time.

Now, let's look at the wrong and the right way to talk to Mr. Denzkogger:

**The Wrong Way**

Denzkogger: "Where the hell are my two dozen Ultra-Glide No Stik Pizza Paddles? I ordered them seven weeks ago!"

You: "Well, sir, the company's ordering system sucks and this happens all the time."

Now Mr. Denzkogger is wondering why he is doing business with your company at all, and your boss will shortly be wondering why you work there. This is counterproductive.

**The Right Way**

Denzkogger: "Where the hell are my two dozen Ultra-Glide No Stik Pizza Paddles? I ordered them seven weeks ago!"

You: "You haven't received that order? I'll check it out right away. What's the order number?"

Denzkogger: "19284564436384756328-EX-39547485 87908664430384-9"

You: "Just a moment, sir, while I bring that up on our computer screen."

After rummaging through your desk, your drawers, your files, and yelling down the hall, you finally find the order on the floor.

You: "I have your order right here, sir. That was an order for 24 Ultra-Glides, placed on May 15th."

Denzkogger: "That's right."

You: "Our average delivery time is three weeks, Mr. Denzkogger. This really shouldn't have taken this long. I can understand why you're upset."

Denzkogger: "You're damn right."

You: "I'll look into it and call you back within the hour."

So far you've just revealed what was in Shell Number 1. You then take the order to Jerry in Shipping and beg. Jerry says the best he can do is two weeks. You get back on the phone knowing you can't offer this to Denzkogger without an explanation, so you decide to uncover Shell Number 2.

You: "Mr. Denzkogger, I've found the problem. Your order was misfiled and wasn't sent to the shipping department. I'm terribly sorry. This time I will put it through personally and we can have your Glides out to you in two weeks."

Notice the passive construction, "Your order was misplaced." Notice, too, the switch to the active construction, "This time I will put it through personally." Makes it sound like you had nothing to do with the screw up but will have everything to do with the fix. And you thought English composition was a waste of time.

> Denzkogger: "Two weeks! What's the matter with your outfit! Haven't you guys got your ordering system straightened out yet? Jackson over there told me it was screwed up, but this is unbelievable. I know some of your other clients and they tell me this happens all the time!"

Whoa. Denzkogger's fingers hover over Shell Number 3, threatening to tear away the thin veil of competence to reveal a seething swamp of chaos. Now is the time to breathe deeply, and remember that you do not need to lift up that shell. With a quick flick of the wrist, you twist the shells, and open up Shell 2 again.

> You: "I'm very sorry about all this, Mr. Denzkogger, and as I said, I will personally follow up on your order and make sure it gets to you no later than July 17."

Same info rephrased. Notice the added specifics: "No later than July 17." Specifics make things sound more concrete.

The more you get in the habit of thinking in these shells, the less often you'll get stuck saying things you didn't want to say.

If all else fails, remember the all-purpose bailout: "I'll have to check with my boss on that," or "I'm not that familiar with our company's policy on releasing that kind of information, but I'll check and get back with you."

**You Want It When? Ha, Ha—Uh, I Mean, Yes Sir** Another example of when to use the Shell Game is on delivery dates. Working backwards, in Shell Number 3 you put the time you think you can finish the project if everything goes like it's supposed to. In Shell Number 2, you put the time it will take if the usual stupid problems delay things. And in Shell Number 1, you put the time it will take if deranged terrorists seize your company and hold everyone hostage until the Brady Bunch is reunited.

You start by offering Shell Number 1, a time frame you know you can live with no matter what happens. If your client won't go for that, you can let 'em peek under Number 2 without taking the shell completely up. As explained by our friend Ed, here's how it works:

> I would say, "There's a real good chance we will get it to you by then but I don't want to commit to it because we may not be able to. So in reality, off the record, yeah, we can make it by this date. But officially, I'm going to have to give you this date."

That way your client feels the warm glow of your going out of your way to let them know that little something extra without your having to really nail it down. Before you try this, though, make sure this is a client who won't "forget" that you told them that the earlier date was an estimate, not a vow. Ed says, "I had to feel comfortable enough with them to know that they weren't going to come back to me at a later date and say, hey, you promised it then."

As for Shell Number 3, the time it takes for you to deliver if everything goes right, you shouldn't ever give this information out. I urge you, my fellow Americans, not to undermine this great nation of ours by making a promise you will have to break more often than you can keep.

## Vendors, Or Who's That Guy Salivating in the Corner?

In the section on clients above, I presented a handy little diagram illustrating the attitude you might have toward a client. Here's another, this one about vendors:

Would you mind too much
if I sent you buckets of money?

Let's do some business.
What cool stuff can you do?

I am thy lord and
master, thou wilt obey!

In this one, you also start at the left, but usually just briefly. You want to make sure the vendor isn't the president's sister-in-law or the only one of its kind on the planet. In other words, you ask yourself, "Does this vendor have some special relationship with the company I should know about?" If that checks out, you move to the center position and try to stay there. You move to the right if the vendor is trying to jerk you around for any reason: to get more money, to do a cheesier job that's less trouble for them, or to give you something different than you want. Essentially, you pull rank. If you have to do this too often, you get a new vendor.

Let's take these positions one at a time.

**Would You Mind Too Much If I Sent You Buckets of Money?** Before you do anything with a vendor, find out the vendor's status. If the vendor did business with the company before you came there may be relationships you don't know about. Let's say she's a computer consultant who set up the company's system. If the LAN dies, she may be the only one who can breathe life back into it. In that case, she's got your company by the cables.

Sometimes a company will supply yours with parts you can't do without. Apple can't make a Mac without Motorola chips; Diet Pepsi can't do without NutraSweet. Ed found this out in his business:

> At my company, the components we were getting from the vendors were kind of specific. We didn't have a lot of choices about who to go to, so we were dependent on these guys. When that's the case, there's only so much you can do, because they know you can't just go out and get another one of these things off the shelf somewhere else tomorrow. Depending on how specialized your product or service is, you may need them more than they need you.

In this situation you actually have to be careful not to offend the vendor—the same way you would avoid offending a client. And because the vendor is in the driver's seat, it can cause headaches for you, as Ed found out:

> Sometimes their scheduling was such that it really screwed up our delivery date. We'd promise a client that we could have it done by a certain date, and then our vendor wouldn't come through, and as a result we were unable to keep our promise. And that was a problem, especially for me, because I was in the marketing end of it, making these promises. I was the one who had the relationship with the clients, sticking my neck out there, and then when someone else didn't come through that I didn't have any control over, it made me and the company look bad. Vendors were also notoriously bad, at least in this case, about keeping us updated along the way. They didn't tell you there was a problem until there was a *real problem*. They wouldn't tell you, "Hey, this thing could be potentially bad." It would probably be a better business practice for them to give you a heads-up along the way, and say, "I hope this isn't going to result in a delay, but it's possible we may have to

> push this back," instead of just calling you on the day it's due and saying it's a week behind.

If you've got a vendor like this, you want to know it from the start. That way you can shmooze him up so he'll be less inclined to let you down. And knowing you've got a vendor you'll have to live with whether you like it or not, you can plan to work around him. In Ed's case, he started building really long lead times into his estimates.

Sometimes you're stuck with a vendor not because they're the only ones that make the 3.5-millimeter fergleknocker but because they're just so damn important that everybody in the field has to stay in their good graces. One worker says this about some of the consultants she has to deal with:

> Yes, we're spending money on these consultants, but sometimes they're fairly powerful in and of themselves. In a way, I need them more than they need me. They're big enough in their field, and I'm counting on the friendship that I've got with them. It's because of the friendship that I'm able to use them instead of someone who's not as good.

Nothing much you can do except kiss butt.

**I Scratch Your Back; You Sell the Company Down the River** When you do this kind of homework, you sometimes stumble into another kind of "special" relationship. A very special relationship. I ran across a couple of these myself.

The first was a vendor who took me out to lunch the first week I started a new job. I'd already checked out his prices and found they were high, so I was inclined to look for other vendors. But Joe didn't want to talk about prices. "You should come down to the plant," he said. "We've got a *real nice* customer facility down there." "Izzat so?" says me. "Oh, yeah, yeah," says Joe, "we've got a whole *suite* there. Got a gym, a pool, a weight room. Hey, you like Acapulco? We've got a condo in Acapulco, just for clients. Ah, it's *beautiful* down there." Now I knew why the guy before me used this vendor. I finished the lunch and never talked to him again.

In this case, the vendor was just bribing my predecessor, so it was easy to fix the problem by chucking the vendor. You might find, though, that your vendor is bribing somebody else in the company. That gets tricky.

I had to deal with that when I used a vendor who had a long relationship with Sam, the guy in the promotions department. When the bill came in for my job, it was outrageous. I went to the vendor and said, "what gives?" Unbelievably, this is what the vendor told me: "Well, last year we did a job for Sam, and we screwed up our estimate on it. It turned out that we lost money on the job. Sam told me we could charge more on this job to make up for it." When I went to Sam, he denied it. After going back and forth between the vendor and Sam, the vendor was forced to adjust his bill. Sam pretended to be as incensed about the vendor as I was, and we agreed never to use him again. But the whole deal stunk like old bologna, and after a few years in the company, it became obvious that Sam had *a lot* of special relationships with vendors. Management got wise, and Sam soon took his last elevator down.

If you run across people in your company who are deep into this, the best thing to do is to act incredibly stupid and naive. Don't acknowledge any hints like, "Well, old Billy Bob offers us a *unique service*. You understand." Don't understand. Act dumb. *Make* them tell you they're a lying pack of thieves. It's amazing how scared chiselers can get if they think they're faced with some insane lunatic who's actually honest. Honesty is dangerous and unpredictable. They don't know *what* the hell you might do, *whom* you might tell, you little fool. And all you have to do to cause this panic is sit there and not get it. Don't agree to cover for them, no matter what.

The next step is to go to someone you trust in the company, and again, act dumb. Start with something like, "I don't know if this is some standard deal I don't know about, but Leo over in Purchasing . . ." The good thing about this approach is that if you're wrong and what you think is an ethical abomination is actually business as usual (and it can be the same thing), you haven't gone too far down the road to sainted martyrdom.

If you finish looking around for any of these special relationships and find none, then it's time to move to the middle, where you'd like to stay if you can.

**Let's Do Some Business. What Cool Stuff Can You Do?** Beginners often make the mistake of starting with the Lord and Master schtick instead of here. It happens like this. The vendor walks in and starts talking technical details. You, not wanting to appear stupid (and realizing she's pulling the Shell Game on you), try to ask probing questions. You're trying to get under Shell Number 2 or 3. The vendor smiles to herself and starts shuffling the shells. You're soon forced into pretending you know what you're talking about, and you start dictating terms. By doing this you stand a good chance of paying big bucks for your little pride ride. The vendor then says, "And of course you'll want the triple-reinforced polyethylene coated grommets on those," and then adds, with a little chuckle, "Would you believe that I have customers that still order the plain grommets? What a bunch of amateurs!" You're left to mumble, "Yeah, amateurs. Of course I'll take those triple poly . . . what you said."

Sometimes a vendor won't even bother with the Shell Game if your naivete plays into their hands. In printing, for example, there are lots of ways to save large amounts of money by adjusting the size of a brochure by a quarter inch. This is because industrial sheets of paper come in particular sizes; if your brochure can be cut out of the master sheet efficiently, it's cheaper. Now if you *command* a printer to make you a brochure that's nine and a quarter inches tall instead of nine (as printers have told me some people do) your friendly printer may just follow your orders and charge you a bundle.

To avoid this, forget about being smart. Admit that you're learning and ask for advice. Let your vendors tell you the absolute coolest stuff they do, and why they think it's cool. Sometimes you'll get some tired geezer who really has no interest, but often you'll get someone who's so flattered and enthusiastic about showing off their knowledge that they'll do a lot of your work for you. Ed found this out:

> They're the experts in the area. That's why they're in that business and that's why you've gone to them. If you treat them as such they'll be more helpful than if you treat them as peons you're just using to get your job done.

If you get a good relationship going with a vendor, she will be willing to do all kinds of things for you: write up reports you can use, get information, and, on occasion, save your tail. For example, you might have a great idea to present to the boss, but you don't know what it'll cost. A vendor who knows she has your respect will be willing to work out the details and cost even though she knows the project might never happen. She will even watch your back for you, catching your mistakes. I once had a printer who would stop the presses if he saw a major typo, like a wrong date—something that was not his responsibility but which saved my butt many times. A vendor you're just *using* won't waste his time.

**I Am Thy Lord and Master; Thou Wilt Do My Bidding**
Of course, some vendors will think your benevolent attitude makes you a pushover. If your vendor starts trying to call the shots, you've got to ever-so-politely suggest that you are in charge.

This usually seems harder than it actually is. Vendors aren't stupid. They know you hold the purse strings—unless they've been cozying up to the boss, which is a different matter. In that case, go to your boss and let her know what's going on.

Don't feel like you have to start the conversation with, "Just who the hell do you think you are, buddy?" Try dropping clues that get your point across, like, "Well, that option might be a better deal as you say, but it doesn't meet our company's needs," or "I know this will be new for you, but I've been asked to get an itemized bill for each project from now on," or "We've been happy with your work but from time to time we need to check the market out there, so we'll be sending this project out to bid." That last line will quickly throw the fear of God into a vendor. In a nice way, you're saying, "You're back to square one." If a vendor won't shape up, it's time to go a-shopping.

## Shop till *They* Drop

The idea behind finding good vendors is to let them do the work. There are two standard approaches. The first is to send a job out to bid, and the other is to send out a Request for Proposal (ubiquitously referred to as an RFP).

With a bid, you have a specific thing you need to buy or to get done. You send out the specs to a bunch of vendors and they send you back what it's going to cost. You can do this with phone calls if you're in a hurry, but the problem is that you'll sometimes find yourself changing what you want as you go along, so by the time you call the last vendor you've got him bidding on a completely different job than the first vendor. The best thing to do is to use the phone to gather some basic information, decide what you want, and then send out a letter and spec sheet. When you find a vendor that looks good, you give them the job and see how they do.

A variation on the bid process is to instead tell vendors how much you can spend, and then see what they can give you for it. This works well if you're trying to get the most out of your budget. It's also great for getting an education. When you get the bids back, have the sales reps come in and explain their bids. You can pull out the competing bids and say, "Yours looks pretty good, but Big Banana Bags will give me triple-reinforced polyethylene-coated grommets for the same price. What's the deal?" To which the competing vendor may reply, "Are you kidding? Those grommets are *garbage*! The coating melts in the first spin-dry and then they pop like twist-offs from a six-pack." You have to compare a lot of conflicting claims, but eventually you get a feel for who's true and who's bogus.

A Request for Proposal is a different species. Here you're usually looking for a range of services rather than a specific job, and there is usually a time span attached, like a yearly contract. Companies often use RFPs when they're looking for an ongoing relationship, like an advertising agency or telemarketing company. Like bid variation number two above, an RFP will typically specify the dollar amount. It's up to the proposer to propose the most bang for the buck.

RFP's come in all kinds of styles, but the stuff you want to know about falls into a few general areas:

**Background on the company** This is where they tell you what's so special about them; why they think they can do a good job.

**Approach to the project** The general way this company plans to solve the problem. An ad agency, for example, might say, "To reach your target audience, we believe strongly that this campaign should avoid the use of television and radio advertisment and instead utilize a fleet of highly trained Dobermans packing sandwich boards through the financial district."

**Past successes with similar projects** Here you find out how much experience they've got in this particular kind of job.

**The plan** The details of how they're going to do what they say they're going to do. This can be pages and pages of technical descriptions, tables, numbers, etc., or just a few pages of prose, depending on the project.

**The people** Information in this section can range from short bios of the vendor's people who'll be working on your project to a list of new positions the vendor will create and fill to work on your account, the key staff involved, their complete resumes, and the percentage of the time they'll devote to your project.

**The schedule** How long it's going to take, and what's going to happen when.

**The cost** This is usually itemized in whatever level of detail you ask for.

Some people get very specific with their RFPs. They require the vendor to submit a proposal with a table of contents, with certain things in certain sections and in a certain order. They want costing that accounts for every paper clip.

If you think you need to send out an RFP, look over a few that other people in your company have put out—that should give you the general idea.

The secret to comparing companies once you get all the material back from vendors (whether from bids or from RFPs) is to let them clear up any confusion you have. If two vendors seem close but you can't understand the features they're talking about, call them up and ask them to explain it or to submit more information.

## Will You Be My Instabuddy?

If you're in a position to dole out money to vendors, it won't take long for them to call you up / knock on your door / send you letters / shake your hand / "Hey, how you doing?" / "What a great office you have!" / "You want to go to lunch?" / "Would you be my *very best* friend?"

You might have vendors descending on you even if you don't directly control the cash flow. If a vendor perceives that you might have something to do with purchasing, you're a target. When Ed was an estimator for an engineering firm, he was approached all the time, even though it wasn't his call:

> There were times when the other estimators and I would sleaze in a free lunch, but that was as far as it went. This sales guy would say "Hey, let's go out to lunch and talk about this," and we'd say O.K., and we'd get there and *then* we'd say, "Here's the guy you gotta talk to." But that was a lot—knowing the right person to call. It was worth it to them, and to us, too.

Sometimes this can get out of hand. The great majority of vendors would never offer an out-and-out bribe, but some will try to get their clients hooked on perks—tickets to events, boating trips, vacation cabins, stuff like that. There's no standard line where these freebies turn from gifts of appreciation to buy-offs. The biggest spiff I ever took was two tickets to Cirque du Soleil. I didn't feel bad about it because it was from a company that had just won a three-month contract from us. I wouldn't have accepted if they'd offered *before* we had decided who to award the contract to.

Some companies have hard-and-fast rules about what you can accept and what you can't. Although accepting a free lunch is almost universally O.K., there are some companies that are very strict. Often these are government offices. When new ethical guidelines came down at the city of Los Angeles, as nearly as anyone could tell, city employees couldn't even accept a *donut*.

If your company doesn't have any guidelines, you just have to go on your instinct. The test is simple. If you'd feel bad firing a vendor for any reason *besides* business—because he's so thoughtful, buying you a bottle of the good stuff on your birthday; buying your nephew's raffle tickets; getting those great seats for the playoffs—you've got a problem. If you can go to the playoffs tonight and fire his butt tomorrow because he botched a job, you're probably all right.

## The Customer Down the Hall

When I mentioned internal clients and vendors earlier I wasn't talking about those little voices inside your head. I'm talking about people inside your company that you should treat like clients and vendors. The bigger your company, the more likely you'll have people like this.

As I said, outside the company clients and vendors are distinguished by the money flow. Inside the company, they're distinguished by the *information flow*. People you deliver information to—in the form of projects, facts, reports, little yellow sticky notes—those are your clients. People who give information to you are your vendors.

The idea is to take all the stuff I said about clients and vendors and apply it inside your company when appropriate. If you've got somebody to whom you always give information, then you can treat them like a client, even using the shell game when necessary but paying special attention to setting up a delivery schedule with plenty of leeway. Just because this person is inside the company doesn't mean that you should be so wildly irresponsible as to say, "If everything goes just right I'll get it to you in two weeks." Go ahead and pad your time, and don't feel bad about it. It's called contingency planning. Remember that if you screw up with an outside client, they go away, but if you screw up too much with an inside client, you go away. When you've got an inside vendor, follow my vendor advice. Don't just try to get what you need; ask them what they think you could use.

When the people you work with switch from clients to vendors, just switch your attitude. Get in the habit of associating your outlook with the job being done, not the person.

# PART 2

# What You're Supposed to Do

Chapter 4

# In Your Face: The First Weeks

OH MY GOD! YOU'RE ACTUALLY IN AN OFFICE WORKING. YOU'RE ACTUALLY SUPPOSED TO KNOW WHAT YOU'RE DOING. NOW WHAT? GET A GRIP. YOU CAN'T BE EXPECTED TO FOCUS YOUR EXCEPTIONALLY ANALYTICAL MIND WHEN YOU HAVE TO GO TO THE BATHROOM AND YOU DON'T KNOW WHERE IT IS. OR WHAT'S GOING TO HAPPEN DURING THE COFFEE BREAK. OR IF YOU CAN WANDER DOWN THE HALL AND JUST CHAT, LIKE YOU DID IN YOUR DORM.

You learn all this stuff by being socialized in your first few weeks at work. In this chapter I'll try to do two things: make you aware of the process of adopting new behavior and inform you of the kinds of behavior you'll probably be expected to adopt.

# You, Me, and Margaret Mead

You're about to be socialized because, as I said in the introduction, you've just joined a tribe. No matter how much it seems like a coolly rational civilization on the surface, you can be sure that just below throbs ritual, superstition, passion, blood loyalties, and magical thinking. To be a fully respected member, you'll develop and grow into the secret ways of your tribe just as every other member has. But to see even more deeply into what it all means (and to learn it faster), you should also take the view of an anthropologist studying the peculiar ways of these people. Let me stress that just doing one or the other doesn't work.

If you simply soak up the culture without thinking about it from some kind of objective point of view (postmodernists, hold your tongues), then you'll chant the same chant and dance the same dance as all the other shamans. One of the best things you have to offer is the much-ballyhooed "fresh perspective"—and you can only put that into play if you ask some tough questions and doubt some general wisdom.

On the flip side, if you insist on analyzing everything to death and loudly shouting "This doesn't make sense!" every time something doesn't make sense, you will anger the devout. Many things in life do not make sense, my child. A good part of you should be prepared to wallow in your humanness and the humanness of your fellow workers.

O.K., you be Joseph Campbell and I'll be Margaret Mead. What? You want to be Claude Levi-Strauss? All right, go ahead. Here we have a few bits of ethnography brought back from the field:

**Myths and Legends** It has been noted that these tribes have their own sacred stories. Keep your ears open for stories and explanations people tell that carry extra weight. These might be about people, such as "Noodleman *knows* his extruded plastics. *Everybody* remembers when he sold Myers

Industries on replacing their steel caster housing with polystyrene." Or it might be an oft-repeated excuse, such as "If those government toadies would just leave us alone we might be able to get some work done around here!" When somebody repeats a myth or legend, everybody else chimes in or nods in agreement. That's how you know it's mythical.

Another mythical form is the reason given behind a particular activity that the company does. For example, there may be an employee newsletter that is completely ignored by the employees. Management will tell you that it's published to give the employees information so they don't have to rely on the grapevine. Like hell. The newsletter doesn't run information; it's there to print company propaganda. Besides, any good gossip will flash through an office long before a staff writer can gather all the information she'll be leaving out of the official story. So why the waste of ink? Because it reinforces a myth management needs to believe: that they are doing something to control unsanctioned information.

Analyzing company myths like these can tell you a lot about what your tribe admires and what it fears.

**Written Rules Everybody Ignores** Disregarding policy is a common practice among the indigenous peoples of the bizworld. For instance, the employee manual might be the Ten Commandments of your company, or it might be something akin to *Miss Manners' Guide to Etiquette* for the 1960s. It's more likely to be the latter. To find out, flip through the pages until you find a rule that's not obvious. The rule that says "employees shall arrive ready for work at their assigned time" is way too obvious—but don't pick one that's too obscure, either.

Let's say on page eighteen there's a rule that says there will be no gum-chewing at one's desk. Over the next week or so, casually ask several people about the rule, and how strictly it's enforced. The reactions you'll get will tell you how closely the employee manual is abided by. If people tend to say,

"Management sticks to that one" or "Nah—that's in there, but no one pays any attention to it," then you know the manual is read and holds some clout—even if the particular rule you picked is outdated. If people tend to say, "What manual?" then your question is answered.

Your company may have a zillion policies, only one-tenth of which anyone pays any attention to. Using this trick you should be able to sort the live ones from the duds.

**Pathological Organization, or My Datebook Is Fuller Than Your Datebook** People in organizations place a very high premium on, well, organization. Their files are tidy, their desks are neat, and everything in their offices is set at right angles. Of course, when you need to work on the Jenkins account there is a practical value in being able to *find* the Jenkins account. But beyond this there is a mystical value associated with neatness. The box is a religious icon in the tribes of bizfolks. The in box. The out box. The boxes on the organizational chart. The little boxes on a calendar. Bizfolks feel that if you put something in a box you have contained its spirit; you have partially neutralized its potential for bad magic.

The more boxes you have at your command the more powerful you will be perceived. Planners, tables, and charts are all strong medicine. Datebooks, or organizers, are at the very vortex of this spirit world. To come to a meeting or a one-on-one discussion without your datebook is like Luke Skywalker without the Force.

**Your New Tongue** Within the general root language of biz speak, each tribe has its own dialect. Very often these will be rife with jargon and acronyms. Now you might be thinking, "So I have to learn a few new terms. How hard can that be?" Let me tell you, when talk is going by at sixty miles an hour, it can be tough.

One place I worked (Commuter Transportation Services, Inc., referred to by its acronym CTS, of course) will offer a good example. Here's the kind of conversations we had there:

> "Did you hear about the CMP Irvine adopted? The TROs are driving the private sector bonkers. ETCs have to try to get their AVRs way beyond reg fifteen levels."
>
> "Are there any strong TMAs out there that can help?"
>
> "OCTA hasn't supported their formation. They're hoping the new HOV lane on the 57 corridor will solve the problem."
>
> "Was that built with ice tea money?"
>
> "No. RCTC, OCTC, LACTC, VCTC and AQMD."
>
> "See what Bill at SCAG thinks."
>
> "He's out today. He's on a nine-eighty. Besides, he's not a big TDM fan."
>
> "All right. Let's try to increase placements by sending updated matchlists to all registrants."
>
> "You're a genius, boss."

Even if you're able to realize from context that RCTC, OCTC, LACTC, VCTC and AQMD are all government agencies that funded the HOV lane (High Occupancy Vehicle lane, or, in simple terms, a carpool lane), I'll bet you're still stumped by "ice tea money." Ice tea is the pronunciation of ISTEA, which stands for the Intermodal Surface Transportation Efficiency Act, by which the federal government is authorized to give money to local governments. Fascinated as you must be by this discussion, I'll refrain from taking time to explain all the other jargon in that little exchange. Just realize that it's all real. Trust me.

So what do you do when people start zipping off in this direction? Just listen, and ask questions later. Don't be in a hurry to use jargon. Sometimes there are shades of meaning you won't get right away, and shooting your mouth off will just make you seem like a wannabe. Take your time, and ask people to explain. They'll love to, because they'll get to display all their hard-earned inside knowledge to the neophyte.

Don't pretend you know a word even if you have the sinking feeling that it's a term you should have remembered from school. In that case, just say something like, "I know I've heard that term before, but I can never remember it's precise meaning." Even if the person you ask *does* think you're an idiot for asking (which is unlikely), at least you've only made yourself look like a dope in front of one person instead of going around for the next several weeks using the word when everyone knows you don't know what the hell you're talking about.

**Magazines, Publications, Professional Associations**
One way to get acquainted is to read what the tribal elders read. Most fields have professional associations that put out some kind of publication, either a magazine or a newsletter. Copies are probably lying around the office. Pick them up and just start reading, even if it's boring and you don't understand what they're talking about. If you do this enough you'll find floating bits of knowledge beginning to attach themselves in your brain when people around you talk. For example, someone might say, "Lou Finster is speaking at the convention this year." You comment, "I was reading in *Ball Bearing Update* about the Finster Roll-o-Matic. Is that the same guy?" Whether the answer is yes or no, your compadres will be impressed that you're reading the trades.

**Can We Talk? I Don't Think So** If you want to talk to your friend Lisa, you probably just call her. If she's not home, you leave a message for her to call you back so you can talk. If Lisa worked in an office three doors down, you might just strut over and say hi. If she wasn't there, you'd just drop by later.

This works fine for normal human affairs, but in business—especially now that everybody's plugged in to something—it doesn't work at all. People in business are often out of their offices, either schmoozing a client or in some endless meeting. You can't wait to talk to them directly, especially for projects that require *immediate* give and take. Instead you have to get used to giving long, detailed messages on voice mail, e-mail, or faxes. Expect to get long, detailed messages back. And to follow-up with more long, detailed messages. That's how the tribes do it. Smoke signals for the 90s.

When you first arrive you might be a victim of the "Tag, you're it a hundred times" game. It's a variation on telephone tag. What happens is someone has a long list of stuff they want you to do, but they don't want to tell you directly because they'll seem too bossy, and besides, you might tell them to go pluck turkeys. So they call when they know you won't be in and leave the bucket o' work on your voice mail. Lunch is a good time, but the real Tagmeisters call from their home at nine o'clock at night. On top of dumping a load on you, they create the impression that they're good soldiers, working long into the night. This allows them to tell their boss, "I'm just waiting for that new guy to get back to me with what I need." The only real defense against this is to call them back when they're not in and tell them (nicely, of course, and with a rash of well-thought-out reasons) to go pluck turkeys. This is an example of why you have to get good at this long message stuff.

We'll be talking more about communication in these pages, coming soon in a chapter near you. I wanted to tell you about this particularly nasty trick just in case you just got your job, panicked, and turned immediately to this section.

**Casual Day** This custom seems to be sweepin' the nation. It's one day a week, usually Friday, when everybody can come to work in casual clothes. It's presented as a perk, a day when you can relax and not worry about proper business attire. Personally, I think it was invented by an elitist who realized that when everyone dresses for success, you can't tell the princes and princesses from the plebeians. So you get them to come in their hang-arounds so you can chuckle up your sleeve at the bad taste and tacky aesthetics on display. (Am I cynical, or what?) If I were you, I'd be *more* careful about what I wore on casual day than on a normal work day. One Alice in Chains T-Shirt is liable to have the place buzzing like a hive.

## Initiate Me, Baby

Now that you've spent some time as an observer, it's time to become a participant. Time to enter that sweat lodge, don that ritual mask, walk those hot coals. Below, in no particular order, are the rituals and routines you'll need to adopt in the first few weeks. Follow them and be well.

## Eight Ways in Which the Time-Space Continuum Must Be Dealt With in Business

**Summertime, and the Livin' Is Cheesy** The first thing to realize when you come to work is that you are entering at a particular season. I don't mean winter, I mean a season within the company's (usually) yearly cycle. You might arrive three weeks before the end of the fiscal year when everybody's going crazy trying to "make their numbers." You might think it's like that all the time, and so you might panic and start updating your resume before you're there a week. Or you might arrive when the onslaught is over and it's pretty cushy. You might think, "Hey, so what's all this I hear about *working*?"

The cycles might not be immediately evident when you walk through the door. When I worked for a college, I thought July and August would be time to chill. I found out that those months are killers, because that's when you have to prepare for the rush of students in September. September was actually pretty kick-back. So whenever you arrive, don't assume that's how it always is. Talk to somebody who's been there awhile, and they can give you the low-down on the whole year.

All of which answers the question, "When am I going to start to feel comfortable around here?" In most companies, you'll only really start to feel better after the first year, when you see things come around a second time.

**I Was, Uh, at the Client's** Some companies have elaborate systems for keeping track of who's in and who's out. If yours doesn't have a board with little magnets or some such thing, you're lucky. But be aware that people will want to know where you are anyway. Nothing bothers a boss more than hiring somebody and then not being able to find him.

Some places are very casual about errands—you can walk out the door and say, "I'm just going to pick up my dry cleaning. I'll be right back," and that's fine. At other places you'll get a look like, "What do you mean, *dry cleaning*? You're supposed to be *working,* for God's sake." At those places people squeeze their errands in over lunch or when they're out doing some sanctioned business travel. As usual, just watch what everybody else does and don't make any sudden moves.

Depending on your situation, you might not have to tell your boss every time you go to the snack bar for a coke. Just let people around you know.

**Punching the Clock, I Mean, Time Sheet** Some places have time sheets, where you mark down how much time you worked, usually by category—project, client, or funding agency. All those little boxes are enough to give any new worker the jitters. Relax—they're always a pain, but there are always tricks. During your first week *ask everybody you can* about how they fill out their time sheet. Learning the slide-bys here is very important so you don't drive yourself nuts recording every seventeen and a half minutes that you worked on the Nerdman Software account.

**I Told You *Never* to Call Me Here, Usually** Unless somebody tells you otherwise, you can usually make any call you need to for business. Some companies are weirder than others about this, though; they may make you go through the bill at the end of the month to determine which calls were for which clients. For your first few weeks, be conservative in your long-distance calling if you can, until you know what the deal is.

Personal calls are a different thing. You can get a nasty surprise here if you don't know what your company's tolerance is for these. Notice I said *tolerance*, not *policy*. Personal calls are usually an *it's O.K. within limits* deal. To find out the limits, you can call willy-nilly and suddenly turn around to see your boss glaring down at you while you're trying to get concert tickets, or you can watch your cohabitators and see what they do first. If you don't see anybody else making personal calls, it doesn't mean they don't; it just means it's more covert where you work. Follow suit.

**Homework 101** Contrary to what you might think (and what others may tell you), I think if you want to get the boss to let you work at home occasionally, the time to suggest that idea is near the beginning of your employment. If she reacts as if it's the most outrageous idea in the world, you'll be excused because you're just an ignorant newcomer. In a month your boss will have forgotten all about it.

The way to suggest it is casually. Don't act like it's a suspicious activity from the start: "Listen, Ms. Jacobs, I *swear* I will work really hard and won't skip out early or watch TV or anything, *I swear to God*." Be off-handed but direct, and pick a defined chunk of work so you can return with tangible results: "Ms. Jacobs? You know, I've got all these reports to go through, and I wondered if it would be all right with you if I spent a day at home reviewing them." Don't elaborate; assurances will just have the tendency to remind her of all the ways you could shirk your duty if you wanted to.

If she says yes, when you spend that day at home think of some work-related excuse to call her *twice*. Ask for her help or guidance on something. It's especially good if she has to call you back. When you pick up the phone on the first ring it'll make her feel that you're accessible and not off in the void somewhere.

You only need to pull this off once in your first month or two to establish a good precedent, one that you can expand upon later. If you wait too long it will seem like some scheme you just cooked up because you really want to go skiing.

**Homework 102** Don't take work home, or at least don't tell anybody that you're taking work home, unless it's absolutely part of the job. (My editor is smirking at this because she *always* has to take work home. That's one of the things editors have to do.) If you do that at the beginning of your job it will become an expectation, and then a burden, and you'll eventually come to regret it. If you get in the habit of saying to your boss, "I'll look at this over the weekend," soon your boss will begin to say to you, "take a look at this over the weekend." Instead, just say you'll look at it first thing Monday morning. Look at it over the weekend if you want to. On Monday, you'll seem like a quick study.

**Moonlighting** If you've got another job or are planning on getting one, keep your mouth shut about it for the first few weeks. Some bosses are irrationally jealous, to the point where they don't want you doing anything that might drain off some of your brain power. You may find out later that it's no problem. That's fine, but in the beginning, keep it cool.

**Coming Early, Staying Late, or Vice Versa** You've been told when to show up for work and when quitting time is. But you can be pretty sure that that's not the real story. There are extremes on both ends of the spectrum. One teacher I know applied for a job and was told she would be paid for forty hours a week but she would be expected to work fifty or more. Personally I think this should be illegal. On the other hand, I talked to a city worker who said he showed up his first day of work when he was supposed to and found the doors locked. *Nobody* came that early.

Most places are somewhere in between. At some companies where the secretaries arrive at eight, everybody else arrives at ten—but they work into the early evening. At other companies, breakfast meetings at seven are the rage, but people cruise out at four-thirty. Your job is to try to clue in as fast as you can. Keep your eyes open, and you'll figure out what hours are considered acceptable.

For the first month or so you might want to explore those fringe hours beyond whatever your company has as norms for a couple of good reasons. First, it makes you look dedicated and enthusiastic. But more importantly, it gives you a look into an inner circle.

In some offices almost everyone comes in early and stays late, but even where that happens, some people won't be there for those hours. It might be the secretaries, or the folks in the computer department. The absence of these people has the effect of making the others feel more intimately connected, sort of a tribe within a tribe. The smaller the group of extended-hour workers, the more elite they feel.

Often this group is (or considers itself) a power clique who need to feel that they're separate from the rabble. Sarah might come in early carrying a gym bag, just to let you know she's been up for hours already burning off her incredible energy surplus in a predawn aerobics class. A Wall Street worker I talked to said every morning the most senior members would sit at a certain table in the break room. Although it was never specified, you didn't sit there unless you were in that league.

Sometimes after work divides into two times. The first, when all the nonambitious are leaving, the stay-laters will be deeply enmeshed in their project, workin' hard. A half-hour later, they're making the rounds, having chats with the others of their ilk. Not only do they score points for staying late but they get to gather information when people feel more relaxed. Typically, guards will be down, and people will talk more freely. They'll also spend more time talking because, strictly speaking, they're off the clock.

If you want to get a whole new perspective on your workplace, stay late and hang with the late crowd at least a few times during your initiation rites.

## Bunch o' Basics

Let's talk about some real mundane office operations that might throw you just because you'd think they'd be easy to figure out:

**Files** When you arrive, you will probably find that there are a bunch of files waiting for you. They may be from the person you replaced or they may have just been heaved onto your desk from some other department's drawers. If your position had been unfilled for a while, it's likely that your desk was a dumping ground for stuff people didn't know what to do with.

Unless the files are obviously part of a pre-established system that works well, you're better off taking all that stuff and putting it in a separate box and starting your own system. When questions come up, get in the habit of looking through the box; you can then pull what you need, file it with your stuff, and ignore the rest. You can keep the box around as long as you like, but eventually you'll be going to it less and less. After a year, you can send it to the archives or chuck it.

Remember that your files aren't yours; they're the company's. Don't keep sensitive material in there. Some day when you're sick your boss will need the Sniverson report, will go rooting around in the Sniverson file folder and will find your recent letter to Sniverson telling them how much you'd like to work for them and how you've got to get out of the hellhole you're trapped in.

**Paper, Pencils, Floppy Disks, and Other Essentials** This may sound rather motherly, but when you first arrive you should find out who you get this stuff from and *stock up your desk with everything you need.* If you don't, here's what happens: your boss dashes into your cubicle and says "I need you to write a letter to Fargone Industries outlining the main points of that proposal we made up and fax to them on our letterhead instantly. Give me a copy of it on a floppy for my hard drive. Then put the letter in one of those slick binders we have, along with the proposal. Use a yellow hiliter to mark the points in the proposal that you refer to in the letter and Fedex it to them. You'll have to hurry—Fedex closes at five." Instead of spending time composing the letter, you're running around like an idiot trying to find a yellow hiliter. You can spend half an hour trying to collect all this stuff and, worse, not finding it: "Uh, boss, I couldn't find a slick binder. Will this manila envelope do?" The lesson is, keep your desk well stocked with supplies.

**Mail** If there was somebody in your position before you, you'll get mail addressed to them. Unless it's obviously personal, you should open it and deal with it.

Depending on your job, you may get a lot of solicitations to workshops and conferences. Although a lot of this will be junk, mixed in with it may be an announcement for some conference that your company goes to every year. Ask around before you heave it.

You know how at home you get junk mail that's been carefully created to make you think it's from the government? Some business junk mailers use an even more insidious trick: they send something that looks like an invoice. Evidently they're hoping to convince you that you or somebody in your company ordered something you now have to pay for. They hope you will mindlessly send it to the purchasing department. Read carefully.

If you get an ad for a seminar that sounds cool, ask your boss if the company will send you. You may find out there's a company policy that allows a certain amount of the budget to be used for seminars. No one may have told you this because no one wants the new kid horning in on the allowance. By asking about it in your first few weeks you can put yourself in the running. Even if the answer is a flat no, you at least showed an interest in learning more about the biz.

**Keys** A lot of things besides the front door may have keys: filing cabinets, office doors, computers, floppy disk storage. Don't keep these keys on your key ring—keep them some place in the office. Otherwise, someday when you're home sick someone will call you and say the boss wants them to get a file off your computer's hard drive, which they can't turn on without the key.

**The Dress Code** I covered how your appearance affects how you're perceived in the chapter on coworkers. Just to nag you a little more, it's really important that you look sharp in the early days of your new job. If you're a man, that may mean cutting off your beloved ponytail. If you're a woman, it may mean not hanging earrings through all those eight holes you have in your left ear.

No matter how rigid you imagine bizfolks are on this subject, you're probably not imagining rigid enough. We're talking way rigid. I once hired a woman in her twenties who looked very normal—normal hair, light on the makeup, very little jewelry. As far as I could tell, her clothes were completely normal as well—skirts and dresses you'd see anyone wearing at a nice restaurant. Yet one day the head of personnel came to me and said, "I need to talk to you. I think you should sit down with Alice and explain to her that she should be wearing outfits that are a little more *professional.*" I told her I would, but the truth is I had no idea what she was talking about, and I wasn't about to bug Alice. Alice continued to wear her normal clothes, and the personnel director never mentioned it again.

I don't know if she expected three-piece suits on Alice, or what. My only explanation is that when Alice started she was under a magnifying glass; later, she wasn't. I offer this story just to illustrate that people can be *unbelievably* weird about this, so at least for the first six months, play it disgustingly safe.

## Please Help Me—The Fax Machine Has Fallen and It Can't Get Up

And what about our nonhuman brothers and sisters in the workplace? No, I'm not talking about the salespeople. I'm talking about those of the mechanical persuasion.

**Mac Attack** If you work in an office, you'll probably be working on a computer, but it may not be the kind you worked on in school.

You may have worked on an Apple Macintosh in college—it seems to be *the* student computer. If that's the case, you might get a rude shock the first time you sit down to the box the company provides. Nine times out of ten it will be an IBM-compatible, and even if it has Windows (a sort-of Mac style environment) you will still probably have to deal with the underlying operating system, called DOS. That system is confusing and frustrating. You have to type in codes like "CD" or "DIR" into a blank screen to get it to do anything. On top of that, connecting something to an IBM machine, like a mouse, a printer, or a modem, can become a grand headache. You plug in one thing, and something that worked before doesn't work anymore. If you're a Machead forced to work on a DOS machine, don't feel like you're a failure if it gets the best of you. It's not you—they *are* hard to figure out. On the upside, these beasts run tons of software (especially the top business stuff) and they run it fast.

You might also be put down in front of a terminal hung off a mainframe. That is, the box on your desk just sends and gets stuff from the big brain in the cold room down the hall. These things are even worse than working on an IBM in most cases because you're always sharing the power. The system will respond quickly or slowly depending on how many people are using it. They are also typically command-driven and user-hostile.

If you're that rare person who was raised on IBM and now works where Macs are the rule, you don't have anything to worry about—especially if you've used Windows. Macs are easy to learn compared to what you went through with DOS.

Unless you were supposed to know a certain software package as a requirement for your job, don't be afraid to ask for help in learning a new program. A lot of companies have plans in place for that. They may have someone on staff teach you, hire a tutor, or send you to a class.

What about copying software if you've got the same kind of machine at home? I'm sure you know it's a crime. Even if you're using it for job stuff, it's illegal. The idea behind software copyright is that one copy is licensed for one machine. The only exception to this is something called a site license, where, for a big hunk of money, a company or institution can make copies for everyone in the office. Check with the computer person at work to find out before you go copying.

For those of you who after reading that last paragraph think I'm completely out of touch with the real world—yes, I know copying is a way of life for a huge number of computer users. And I further realize that the chances of Bill Gates getting pissed off at you and sending the Microsoft lawyers to nail a summons to your door are pretty slim. After all, you don't have any money.

But business is a different thing. People who run the computer department at a company are *personally responsible* for the use of the software at their company. They can get sued. If you copy software, even if everybody in your department copies the software, *do not tell the computer folks.* Don't even joke around about it. If nothing else, they need what's known in politics as "deniability." They have to be able to say truthfully, "I know of no copying of software at our company."

**Fax Machines and Copy Machines** These wonderful timesavers can waste incredible amounts of time. It's so common to find high-powered executives on their knees trying to yank jammed paper out of a copy machine that the whole subject has become fodder for comic strip artists. If you put something into one of these babies and it breaks, or you fear you broke it, don't waste time playing techie. Just find somebody who knows how to run the thing. In fact, find that person before you even start, so you can learn what you need to know about the particular monster your company has.

## Them Bodily Functions

Now we turn our attention to that which makes us unlike our mechanical friends described above: that we eat, drink, and wear shoes.

**Consuming Freely** It starts with coffee. There's always a lot of activity in the morning around the hot drink deal. Most offices have a coffee machine. At some places the company pays for it and at others there's a coffee club. That's where you pay a few bucks a week, which gives you the right to tank up whenever you want. If you only have coffee once in a while you don't have to join the club; there's the little cup into which you toss your quarter when partaking of the Java. My advice, though, is even if you only have coffee twice a week or just use the hot water for tea, join the club. Otherwise you'll be regarded with suspicion, someone who probably thinks she's too good to join our club, probably a coffee chiseler who steals cups without putting a quarter in and who just doesn't want to help clean the machine when all it takes is a quick wipe with the sponge, the lazy slug.

I hate the word munch, but that's what people do in the morning. If you bring in a box of munchables—donuts, croissants, pastries—that buys a lot of goodwill.

When you're getting your hot liquid beverage and your puffed-up dough confection you'll notice that talk is usually small. Join in. Talk about the weather, sports, gossipy news, TV; ask about family. It's not the time to be RoboWorker; it's the time to wallow in humanness, as I said before.

Same for coffee breaks, which are usually only strictly defined for the hourly staff and float for everyone else. As the day wears on, though, you can ease into worktalk around the water cooler or Coke machine; this is often the best time to bring up an idea casually to somebody who has clout. The psychology works like this: it's not like you called a meeting to pitch this idea—it's just off the top of your head. If it's lame, your listener won't think you put a lot of time into it (even if you did) and will think you're just enthusiastic but green. If it's good, you keep talking, walk out of the break room and into your listener's office where it becomes Real Work.

Next comes lunch. While coffee breaks are egalitarian, a time when everyone from the President to the mail clerk might come together and share a chat, lunch is an exercise in status. In some companies, bringing your lunch is the mark of a peon, and eating it in the company lunch room is quite déclassé. And I can practically guarantee that if you bring stinky leftovers from home in a Tupperware container, zap them in the microwave and eat them in the lunch room while reading *People* magazine, you will never make vice president.

Among the yupscale workers there can be a variety of lunch strategies, depending on the local tribal culture and the theories of the particular luncher. Some have a sandwich delivered so they can keep on a-workin'. Some bring small bits o' food like celery, carrot sticks, or granola bars and "graze" all day long so they can keep on a-workin'. (Although grazers bring stuff from home, it's seen as having more class than brown-bagging lunch.) For some, every lunch is a meeting of some kind with somebody, either inside or outside the company. Some hang with a particular clique every day. Some disappear and read, the antisocial snobs. (That's what I used to do.)

I can't advise any one activity among these, because, as I said, it depends on what you think will work in your environment, although it's probably safest for the first few weeks to join your closest coworkers for a jaunt to a nearby eatery, which they will probably suggest when you're new. After that people will revert to their normal routines.

When you go to that lunch with coworkers or your boss, it's like being on a first date. Don't slurp your pasta. In fact, skip the pasta; it's a mess to eat. Don't get anything too heavy or expensive; you'll feel like a hog by the time you roll out of there. Salads are safe. And don't get beer or wine, even if your boss does. Later, when you know what everybody thinks about it, you might be able to knock one back. Once, after a particularly important press conference, the president of the company I was working at took the staff to a bar and ordered a pitcher of brew and glasses all around. Who was I to say no?

Aside from coffee breaks and lunch, the next most common face-stuffing event is the office birthday party, wedding fete, or baby shower. No big trick here; just smile and eat your cake. Refusing cake, no matter how good your reason ("I go into convulsions if I come into contact with wheat flour"), will be seen as antisocial. Just so you know.

**Nature's Call** You've no doubt heard of the Executive Washroom, that legendary lavatory where only the anointed relieve themselves. I personally have never worked in a place that had one, and in my own naive way I hope they are a thing of the past. People I talked to hadn't seen them where they worked, either.

Bathroom talk is like coffee break talk. Since you can run into any level of person in there, it can range from casual conversation to the pitching of an idea you want to sound casual.

Bathrooms are a good place to hide if you just can't take it for a few moments. A friend said she used to work at a place where some of the secretaries would go into the woman's bathroom, have a seat on the built-in chaise, and have lunch. I used to go to the men's room and take a book.

**Women's Zapatos** In some offices, it's normal for women to have two kinds of shoes: the good-looking pair and the comfy pair. You can stay in the comfy ones in your office and then put on the good pair for clients. Take a look and see if this is the case for you.

**Lighting Up** If you smoke, just quit it, will you? The latest trend is smoke-free offices, so the puffers have to stand around outside the building, where the merciless grip of their addiction is on display for all to see. It's just one more way to be disenfranchised, although in meeting other smokers you might find a pretty interesting crew (I always did when I was a smoker). If some power person is a smoker, I suppose you could take up smoking so you could get closer to him or her—but then there's that little detail of keeling over dead a dozen years early with a black lung—all of which seems to be a drawback. I dunno—you decide.

**Hurling** If you feel bad, go home, especially if you have to barf, you've got a hacking cough, a dripping nose, or something else gross. You won't be able to think straight, and you'll damage your reputation as a sharp, alert worker. Some people think they're showing great dedication by sneezing their way through the day, but that's way overrated. Your fellow workers would rather make do without you than to have you there sick as a dog, believe me.

## The Grand Pageant of Human Existence

A lot of the time you'll spend at work will be spent just hanging out. Here are a few tips.

**Morning!** I covered most of the morning ritual under the section above that talks about coffee. I'll just add that even outside the coffee room, coffee room socializing takes place for the first, oh, half hour or so of work in most offices. Take part and be sincere.

**Visiting** Get out of your cubicle once in a while and just walk down the hall and pop in on somebody else. In most offices, this is acceptable behavior. Ask an open-ended question like, "So, what's up with you?" Whether it's a work answer or a personal answer, just follow the lead and see where it takes you.

If it's a work answer, sometimes you'll find yourself blue-skying, thinking up all kinds of great ideas or solutions, or finding out something that has a major impact on what you're doing. If it's a personal answer, you'll sometimes find that you have something unexpected in common with this person. ("Oh, your house was destroyed in the earthquake? What a coincidence—so was mine!") It can create a bond that will make work go more smoothly.

People who don't visit get a reputation for only showing up when they want something from you or when they've got a problem.

**Life in a Cubicle** If you have a cubicle instead of an office with a door, you better learn quick that those three-inch partitions will give you a very false sense of security. Not only can people walk in at any time and catch you playing Street Fighter II on your computer, but everyone can hear everything you say. I was standing in my cubicle one day when I heard Janice in the next cube talking about my recent promotion. "Now that Garrett's made manager, he's going to move me into his old position. And frankly, I think I'll do a better job, because I'm more organized." I looked over the top of the partition and said to her, "You know, you're right." Luckily, Janice and I were cool with each other. Your boss might not be.

**The Door Question** If you're lucky enough to have a real office with a door, you should realize that closing your door is typically interpreted among the bizworld natives as carrying meaning. The idea that you're simply trying to work without the distraction of all the hallway chatter doesn't occur to them. They just *know* that you're in there (a) goofing off, (b) talking about them behind their back, (c) in there with your boss who's chewing you out, (d) taking drugs, or (e) whatever else is implausible but exciting.

If your office has one of those skinny windows next to the door as a lot of them do, this is less of a problem. It at least stops fellow workers from imagining that you're having sex in there. Still, unless you really need the privacy, keep the door open.

**Choose Your Friends** When you first arrive, there will be the temptation to hang with the first crowd or person you feel good about. Not a good idea. For all you know, they may be regarded as nice but incompetent and soon to be fired. Or deadwood. Or troublemakers. These are reputations you can't know until you've been around awhile, so for starters, be friendly but don't lock on to anybody too quickly.

## How to Act on Your Honeymoon

When you first start a job you've got a clean record and the confidence of your boss. On one hand, you've got to be careful not to blow the faith people have in you when you start out. I hope the section above will help you avoid the biggest blunders. On the other hand, *you must not wimp out.* Settle into wimpdom now, and there will be no turning back. Check it out:

**Go for It** Be aware that you'll be up against the attitude that says new hires shouldn't try too hard. Here's how one vice president expressed it to me:

> People in their twenties are there to just crank the work out. They're not wanted for their decision-making ability. They may be wanted for their analytical skills, but only for very defined situations. It's not the big picture.

The reason managers say this is that their experience shows that most new graduates who try to contribute to the big picture offer the most ignorant, insipid ideas. Not only is this not helpful, it's a pain. In general, these managers are right.

So why am I telling you to do it anyway? Two reasons. First, that old saw is true: you've got to believe in yourself. Your ideas aren't stupid; they aren't like all those other graduates'. *Their* ideas may be lame, but *yours* are not. You may feel intimidated now, but, hard as it may be to believe, you will become more intimidated later as you learn about all the policies, problems, procedures, and general bullshit that stops good ideas from ever seeing the light of day. Throw your ideas out there, and let them get shot down if that's what's going to happen. And then throw out some more ideas. That way you'll begin to feel there's no shame in getting an idea rejected, and your confidence will grow with the ideas that are accepted. If you wait until you think you have the *perfect* idea and can present it at the *perfect* time to the *perfect* people—how absolutely perfect will be the devastation of your ego when they all shout, "Next!"

The second reason is that during your first few months your enthusiasm is high and your knowledge is low, and everybody knows this. Their understanding and tolerance of your harebrained schemes are, therefore, at an all-time high. When they shoot down your ideas, they'll use a pop gun instead of a bazooka. Like a muscle, your self-assurance gets stronger when resistance increases gradually.

So what do you get if you follow my advice and go the risky route? Aside from the aforementioned rise in confidence, you have a good chance of contributing ideas that work. And because ideas that work are rare, and rarer still coming from someone who's been on the job less than a year, you will be held in awe if you can produce even one. The more you can produce, the more freedom and power you'll be given. So go for it.

Sometimes the key to putting this philosophy into action is to not ask permission. When you see a new way to do things that you know will work better—do it before someone tells you not to, because they will if you ask.

When I took a new job and was put in charge of publications, the first thing I noticed was that the company's old publications didn't have a single picture of a human in them. We were a service company, yet there were no people in the brochures.

I decided that we needed to feature the faces of the people who worked for the company. There were two ways I could have approached the project. The first would be to suggest the idea to my boss. She would have no doubt talked to the president. He would have said, fine, talk to personnel and let's see whom we want in the photos. Who's been with the company a long time? Who has been doing an especially good job? And who do we want to avoid? We don't want a picture of somebody on our brochure that we're going to fire tomorrow. As I thought this through, I realized that the whole process would take months, wouldn't give me the best pictures (that depends on faces and expressions, not on good work habits) and also that the whole idea might be scrapped because it would be impossible to be "fair."

I decided to take the second approach, which was to go ahead without asking permission. I simply hired a photographer and had him show up. I didn't even schedule appointments—I didn't want it to get around. Once the camera and lights were set up in an empty conference room, I went from office to office asking people if they wanted to be in a photo shoot. When the photos came back, I asked the art director to choose the ones he liked based only on the quality of the photo.

The result was a brochure with real people in it. As it turned out, the president liked the photos so much we used more of them in the annual report and had a dozen enlarged to poster size and mounted on the offices hallways. In this case, I won the bet.

**Delegate** When you first arrive, you'll probably do a lot of stuff yourself that you shouldn't be doing simply because you don't know any better. At one job I was wrapping my own packages and filling out my own shipping labels before I found out there was a whole crew in the mail room whose job it was to do just that. Ditto for all kinds of paper-shuffling. You don't necessarily have to have your own secretary to be able to delegate. Is there a department secretary who can file stuff for you? Make calls for you? Fax things for you? Since you're new, you may be expected to do it all. But look around first, before you take on all this yourself.

The same goes for more important stuff. If you have to write a report, don't assume you have to do all the research. That's a notion that's proper in college (your work has to be yours) but not in business, where everybody is there to help everybody else. See if it's somebody else's job to provide you with information.

**Perfectionism** This is death in business. Nothing can be perfect, so give it up. Things in business are less perfect than the work you did in college because people produce projects together. Everything's a compromise. In this environment, one person's piece of dreck is another's lovely system. When you try to make something perfect in business, you're working not only against the problem itself but against everyone else's opinion. Hillary put it this way:

> When I came in, I saw the problems, and I decided how I could fix things and make them perfect. But be careful of what you think has to be done perfectly. You'll have to do it and you'll see why other people were willing to let it slide.

Think in terms of percentages: if you can't nail one project 100 percent, go for as high as you can, and realize you'll have a brand new chance to score high on the next project—which will probably be along in five minutes. Try for an attitude of "produce and cut loose."

**I Know That Deep Inside They Know That Deep Inside I'm a Big Phony and Accomplish Almost Nothing Each Day** If you feel like this for the first several months of your job, don't worry. It's normal. It's normal because, for one thing, you're discovering that what you learned in college doesn't necessarily apply to what you do at work. That makes everybody feel insecure. Second, it is sometimes amazing how little work actually gets done in an office—and not because people aren't trying. It happens because the nature of office work is that everybody has to work together (where have I heard that before?). Everybody's got to be on the same beam. Hours, days, weeks are spent just doing that—approvals, meetings, discussions, evaluations—before a decision is made and the action starts. You have to realize that this isn't wheel spinning—it's part of the work. It frustrates everybody, but it's necessary.

As normal as these feelings are, don't blab about your insecurities around the office. Tell your friends outside of work. If you tell your coworkers or your boss, you may convince them that you *are* a phony, and this will not improve your standing.

**Start Collecting Stuff for Your Resume** As anybody who's read a resume book knows, you want your job descriptions to be a list of accomplishments, not duties. The time to begin saving information about what you did is your first day of work.

Start a file and label it "future" or whatever. Make a habit of throwing in anything that serves as documentation or as a reminder of the fine work you did. Copies of memos, reports, even post-it notes—it doesn't matter. Don't try to organize it or categorize anything—this'll be a distraction and make you feel like you have to, and then you'll avoid it. Instead, just toss stuff in. Three years from now when you're ready to put your resume together, you can plow through it. You'll be amazed at the great stuff you'll find that you had forgotten all about.

Chapter 5

# Meetings: Get a Clue

IN THE CHAPTER ABOUT BOSSES, I BROADLY IMPLIED THAT CATEGORIZING IS A WASTE OF TIME, SAYING THAT EVERY BOSS WAS DIFFERENT. BUT THE IMPULSE TO CATEGORIZE IS COMING OVER ME AGAIN, AND SINCE WE'RE TALKING ABOUT MEETINGS HERE, WASTING TIME SEEMS STRANGELY APPROPRIATE. SO HERE ARE A FEW KINDS OF MEETINGS:

**The Weekly Chat** Probably the first kind of meeting you'll be subjected to is a regularly scheduled staff meeting. It might be weekly or monthly, and the staff might be just your department or the whole company, but the nature of these kinds of meetings is the same. Their main purpose is to share information by catching everyone up on what everyone else is doing. Often the meeting proceeds by having each person speak in turn for a few minutes about what they've been doing. A problem arises when these meetings include people from other departments—the people you work with directly already know what you're doing, and the people that you aren't in contact with often don't need to know. But everyone feels compelled to work their jaws for a certain amount of time. If the guy next to you goes on for three or four minutes, then you go on for three or four minutes, even if it's a rehash of something they all know. Every once in a while you'll see somebody who has the nerve to say, "Well, you know what I'm working on, so I'll just pass it on to Phil," but not often enough. The result is a long and boring timesoak you have to endure every week or month. Here's what one manager told me:

> Staff meetings tend to be a waste of time. They don't usually provide new information for the boss, because the boss has gotten the information previously, one way or another. It's really a meeting for the boss to update the staff, but it's presented under the guise that the staff is going to update each other. But most people don't really care what their colleagues are doing.

Even if something important is raised, it's usually not followed up:

> There's a remarkable inability to focus on what other people are doing, even if it's relevant, partially because staff meetings go on so long that nobody wants to ask a question. It's a mistake in big staff meetings to ask a question. It's like, *"No!* It's gonna be another hour! *Stop!*"

So what should you do about staff meetings besides groan a lot? First, be prepared. Try to think of a few things to say ahead of time that sound intelligent and a little different from what you're coworker (who has the exact same job and does the exact same thing) is going to say. Don't come into a meeting cold, even if you know you won't be the first to be called upon, because then you'll be trying to think of what to say during the beginning of the meeting when the boss is talking—and that's the only part worth paying attention to:

> The first ten minutes of the meeting are useful. The rest aren't. It's the eighty-twenty rule. The bulk of it may be worthless, but the twenty percent of it that's useful you can't get unless you're there. It's not the same to ask even a trusted colleague or your boss what happened. You won't get the unfiltered information.

For the remainder of the meeting, watch people closely. What they're saying may be useless, but if you pay attention to how they're saying it and to what they may be leaving out, you can sometimes pick up on undercurrents of political intrigue. You might notice, for example, that Brad isn't bragging about the work he's doing for the Whale O' Fun amusement park. Could it be his project's gone belly-up? Something to keep your ears open for.

This kind of observation can be useful. If nothing else, it's more exciting than drawing doggies on your legal pad.

**The Discuss 'n' Plan** This is your general, everyday, garden variety meeting. It covers a lot of different meetings but has the general quality that meetings are famous for, namely, everyone agreeing that the matter at hand (*any* matter at hand) needs to be looked into more thoroughly—later, by others, as in a committee, or by an entirely different division of the company.

There are a lot of theories as to why this happens. Dozens of books have been written on the problem. Basically, it boils down to this: The point of a meeting is for the majority of the people to agree on what to do, and the easiest thing to agree on is not to agree now—because if that happens, I might not get my way.

Productive Discuss 'n' Plan meetings are either a subspecies (either Brainstorming or Shirtsleeves, discussed below) or manipulated by a smaller group within the meeting that already *had* a meeting in which they figured out how to railroad everyone in this meeting. In other words, some of the people did a Shirtsleeves or Brainstorming and came up with a plan that goes, "When this subject comes up, you say this and I'll say this, then we'll put it to a vote and win. Yea!"

If no one has done this kind of homework, and it's just a free-for-all, the general techniques apply. (See What to Do in Meetings, below).

**The Brainstorm** Many meetings that people call Brainstorming aren't. The object of Brainstorming is to get a lot of ideas on the table quickly, and the rules are simple. For the first part of the session, anyone can offer any idea, no matter how weird. Somebody writes down all the ideas, and *no one is allowed to criticize at all.* That's the crucial ingredient, and the one that's usually ignored. Criticism, no matter how mild, is what stops the flow of ideas.

In the second part of Brainstorming, which is best done after a short break, the list of suggestions is read and everybody evaluates them. The ideas then get culled down to a few useful ones.

What some people call Brainstorming is sitting around and simultaneously thinking up and shooting down ideas. Since it's easier to shoot (and sometimes more fun), people start to spend more time loading ammo and less time putting out targets. The ideas presented are safe. If there are different levels in the room, the honchos hog the floor and the underlings cower in fear.

Another kind of quasi-Brainstorming fails because it's too crowded—say, anything more than about ten people. Typically, they'll go by the rule of no criticism for the first part. Someone will write down the ideas on huge sheets of paper and hang them all over the walls so everyone can see them. The problem is, with a room full of people you feel like you're only going to get one or two suggestions in. You discard a lot of your own ideas before you start. The second problem is that when it comes time to evaluate the ideas, big groups follow the herd instinct and vote for vacuous suggestions like, “Let’s increase productivity.”

If you’re in a fake Brainstorming, don’t bother trying too hard. Because you’re new you’ll just make yourself the easiest target. Just lob a few safe ones their way to show them your hard disk hasn’t crashed.

If you’re fortunate enough to be in a real session, let loose. The more you add the better your chances are of contributing a winning idea—and that will score big points. When Lupé started in advertising (where they know how to Brainstorm) she was in an 8-hour marathon where the group was trying to come up with new product ideas for their client. At the end of the day, although Lupé had only been at the company a few months, all three of the ideas presented to the client were hers.

**The Shirtsleever** Here we have a small group, no more than ten and usually fewer, actually working rather than trying to decide what to do. They may be planning an event, producing the points of a strategic plan, scheduling the dates of a project or coming up with a list of materials or contacts. The attitude in this kind of meeting is that there is no question about what has to be done or how it will be done. It only remains to jump in and do it. This is the kind of meeting that you thought meetings were supposed to be, and you’ll know it when you’re in one.

Sometimes these meetings happen because the people who attend know how to move a Discuss ’n’ Plan into a Shirtsleeves. But often it’s simply because the endless procrastinating that goes on in the Discuss ’n’ Plan has finally ended, decisions were reluctantly made, and now it’s time to work. Often the same people that were such drudges in other meetings come to life in the small, motivated group.

**Hallway Meetings** A little more than ten years ago Tom Peters and Bob Waterman wrote a book called *In Search of Excellence* (Harper & Row), which pretty much started everybody blathering on about excellence. Among other things, the book legitimized something everybody in business felt in their bones: that at least half of the good information you get is not in any formal meeting. It's from talking to Jack at the copy machine, or running into Susan on her way back from lunch, or walking out to the parking lot with Stan. It's happenstance, it's casual, and it's vital. Peters and Waterman popularized it with an acronym: MBWA—management by wandering around. They gave examples of successful companies that encouraged MBWA:

> 3M sponsors clubs for any groups of a dozen or so employees for the sole purpose of increasing the probability of stray problem-solving sessions at lunch time and in general. A Citibank officer noted that in one department the age-old operations-versus-lending-officer split was solved when everybody in the group moved to the same floor with their desks intermingled.

Often these turn out to be the best meetings of all. Here's why:

- When somebody uses casual time to talk business instead of, say, how the Knicks are doing, then they're probably interested in the project.

- They won't start a conversation just to stroke someone—they really need the other person's opinion.

- Because the time isn't scheduled (in fact, they may be on their way somewhere), they'll get to the point fast.

• Also because they're in a hurry, they'll settle quickly on a course of action. "I'll get those figures to you," or "I'll call Jan and pitch the idea to her."

Five things can get squared away and acted on in one of these five-minute hallway meetings, whereas formal meetings can run for hours before people stagger out hoping they never hear about the issues again.

Grab every opportunity you can for a hallway meeting. Before you schedule a formal meeting, see if you can't just find who you want to talk to—right now—especially if it's only a few people. Grab one and say, "Can you come with me over to Larry's office for a minute? I've got this idea I want to bounce off you." It works.

**Show & Tell** Known in the bizworld as presentations, these are the meetings where somebody is pitching an idea or project to someone else. It may be to get them to buy into it, or it may just be to explain it because it will affect others.

Making presentations is an art unto itself—whole books are available on the subject, and if you need to do a lot of presentations, go buy one. For starters, here are a few basics:

• Have something to show • That is, something visual. You'd be amazed at how many people think the best thing to put on the overhead projector is a sheet of paper *with the exact words they are saying*. Filling the screen with your outline, no matter how brilliant, is a waste. You want something that illustrates what you're talking about. A photo of the product, a diagram, a chart, a graph, a table—anything that you can point to and explain.

• Practice with props • If you've got a chart or graph, whether it's posterboard on an easel, a slide projector, or a big-screen computer monitor, practice with it. Even something as low-tech as posterboards can flummox you if you move the wrong way and they all spill on the floor.

• DON'T PASS HANDOUTS AND TALK AT THE SAME TIME • If you've got something you want to give the crowd, make sure it's distributed before you start or after you're finished. If you pass it out while you're trying to talk, no one will be paying attention to you. They'll be talking to their neighbor, looking at the handout, or flipping through the papers. If you're forced to give out your stuff at the beginning, go ahead, but wait until all the shuffling has died down before you start. Don't try to make chit-chat—just wait. When it starts to get quiet, say, "Does everyone have a copy of the sheet I handed out?" If people stop rustling and give you the floor, go ahead. If not, wait some more.

• USE YOUR OWN WORDS • Don't write out everything you're going to say in perfect sentences. Just make an outline that will remind you of the points you need to cover. Then explain the same way you would if there were just one person listening to you.

• KEEP IT SHORT • Fifteen to twenty minutes is plenty. If your audience wants more detail, they'll ask you for it.

• AT THE END, ASK IF THERE ARE ANY QUESTIONS • You're expected to do this, but you might forget, since you're new. Just thought I'd remind you.

## Things to Do at a Meeting

So what is it you should do in a meeting when you're the fresh face? Aside from the particular advice above, here are some general techniques:

**Take Notes** Even if you throw them away when you get back to your office, taking notes looks good while you do it.

**Draw a Map** When you're new, you'll probably walk into meetings without a clear sense of who the people there are. You might know their names and titles, but you might not have had time to figure out their role in this project or their hidden power quotient. Draw a map of the table, and jot down each person's name, what they do, and what they're talking about next to their symbol.

**Jump In Quick** See if you can be one of the first to speak at a meeting. The talkers and listeners are usually established in the first few minutes. You want to be a talker, someone who participates. The easiest way to do this is to ask a question. Try one of these flavors:

• The clarification • One way to stay active in a meeting is to ask someone to clarify something they just said. If you're new, this is especially good, because you can't be faulted for not knowing everything. The classic form is, "Could you clarify what you meant by the phrase 'the boneheaded lawyers'?" By asking you are seen as someone who's eager to understand it all. Just don't ask so much that you're hanging up the meeting.

• The rephraser • Here you repeat what you think the speaker said, rephrasing it or condensing it slightly, and ask if that's what they meant. The classic form is, "So you're suggesting that this year our Northridge retail outlet needs less in the way of sprucing up and more in the way of raising the collapsed roof and imploded walls, is that right?"

• The softball • When Letterman says to Johnny Depp, "So, I understand this film is a change from the kind of roles you usually play. Can you tell us about it?" that's a softball question. Celebs love 'em, and so do bizfolks in meetings. A softball question can perform three functions in one swift move. First, it keeps you in the action. Second, if you ask a higher-up, it makes him or her love you for asking. And third, it's a safe way to derail a conversation that's going in a direction you don't like. The classic form is, "Bob, I understand you've been doing some interesting work in the refried bean division. Can you tell us about it?"

• THE HARDBALL • If you're new, don't try to ask Hardball questions. These are the ones that make someone sweat. You ask them when you want to establish yourself as astute and sharp, but these questions always make enemies. The classic form is, "Your contention that consumers believe Yummer Dums taste 'buttery and smooth' simply does not agree with the report, Mr. Vermin!"

**Follow Your Fearless Leader** If you're in a meeting with your boss, just watch for a while and see what she does. You want to make sure you don't say something in the beginning to preempt your boss's agenda. Here's what Hillary says:

> Once your boss's boss is there, you've got to follow the rules, the implicit rules that your boss wants followed. If your boss isn't raising political issues, then that's not the place to do it.

If you want to contribute, and you're sitting near your boss, suggest your idea to your boss in a side conversation. She can then decide whether to bring it up or not.

**When to Call Your Own Meeting** Wait until you've attended a bunch of meetings before you start calling your own. The best way is to ease into being a meeting monger. Start with hallway meetings, as I mentioned above. Turn them into more formal meetings by asking people if they can get together with you another time to continue the conversation. If you need to arrange something bigger, go to your boss and say you're thinking of getting people together on an issue, and you want to know who he thinks would be appropriate to ask. He'll then help you get things rolling.

## Away From the Ranch

Although they aren't exactly meetings, I thought I'd put in a word about conferences here, since they sound like gigantic meetings when you first hear of them. Like when the National Association of Glue and Adhesive Manufacturers gets together to talk shop in daylong seminars. You sign up and fly to Orlando, really looking forward to Tuesday's seminar: *Epoxy and Its Solvents: An Overview.* You arrive in the late afternoon and roll into the evening event, and everyone seems to know each other already. When everybody's networking hot and heavy, you might feel like a failure. Don't—it takes a few years in any industry before you can really work a schmooze-fest. Hillary has this to say:

> I think going into one of those big ballrooms for the social event, like the cocktail hour, where you don't know anybody, is hard. It's not an environment that's conducive to going up to somebody and saying, "Hi. I'm So-and-So. What do you do?" Everybody's nervous about it. Look for people who seem to be at your level. I wouldn't try to go up and meet the head of X, your competitor, when you're an analyst in company Y. If I were starting out, I would set very low expectations. If you meet one person whom you're going to stay in touch with, great.

And don't expect a lot out of the workshops, either. People of every level of experience go to conferences, so presenters try to offer material that somehow covers everything from the most basic material to the most esoteric. Chances are you'll hear some stuff you already know and a lot you can't figure out. Hillary again:

> Nobody ever gives away trade secrets, but if you're listening to competitors talk you can glean a couple of things. But they're not useful in the surface way they are presented. They're presented to educate somebody on topic A, and they're really useful on a piece of B.

If you wind up going to a lot of conferences, hook up with a friend to make the rounds. That'll get you on the networking track sooner rather than later.

Chapter 6

# Trekking the Paper Trail

O.K., WE'RE NOT STICKING STRICTLY TO PAPER IN THIS CHAPTER. WHAT WE'RE TALKING ABOUT IS COMMUNICATION AND DOCUMENTATION—THINGS THEY USED TO DO ONLY ON PAPER (BACK IN THE PRE-WIRED MISTY AGES LONG AGO) BUT NOW DONE ON SCREEN, ON-LINE, AND BOUNCED OFF SATELLITES.

There's a difference between something composed and something spewed off the top of your cerebellum. And there's a difference between hard copy and flashing phosphors, between something said in the corner booth at Señor Margarita's and a comment digitized and resting in the bowels of voice mail.

## Five and a Half Ways to Communicate That Are Better Than a Message in a Bottle

Sharp bizfolk never make a call or churn out a memo without considering how the form fits the content. They consciously think about the kind of message they're delivering, whom they're giving it to, and the reaction they want and expect. Then they pick the medium that's going to do the best job—in person, phone, voice mail, e-mail, or paper.

Let us ponder for a moment the essences of these media and what works best for each situation.

**Live and In Person** The most fundamental communication channel is face-to-face conversation. You've got your mouth moving, your eyes rolling, your arms flapping—there's much more going on than just the words. This channel has the slick double advantage of being the most immediately compelling and least recordable means of persuasion. That means if you want to swing somebody over to your side by appealing to emotion and loyalty, don't write them a memo—at least not to start. Go pay them a visit. It's also best if you've got to cool a hothead down or pitch an idea that you might get an iffy reaction to. In person, you can answer questions and adjust your words and moves according to the slightest twitch of your listener's eyebrow. The drawbacks are that you have to think fast and hit your marks the first time or you turn into a blathering moron saying, "I didn't mean to say that the *whole* report sucks, I mean, some parts don't suck—much, I mean . . ."

**Ma Bell Straight** Next in line is the phone call. Pouty lips or obscene gestures aren't available for that little extra emphasis, but you've still got your authoritative voice and the ability to counter objections, and you can even be reading from notes if you need to—which looks kind of lame in a heated face-to-face discussion. Unless your company has some perverse policy about recording calls (some do, mainly for customer service), your phone calls, like personal conversations, melt into the ozone when you're done. Use the phone for fast info, subjects that aren't too sensitive, and to renew connections. Once again, the strengths of using the phone: emotional and nontraceable.

**Ma Bell à la Memorex** Next we move on to voice mail, that hybrid animal. You can still ladle on the emotional twang, but now you've got to do some composing—in your mind if not on paper—and your message is left as evidence. Although there's not a hard copy hanging around, on a lot of voice mail systems the message can be easily copied and sent to anyone—or everyone—in the company.

One of the main advantages to voice mail is you can talk to somebody without bothering to listen to all their annoying questions and comments. This comes in handy, as I pointed out in Chapter 4, for making requests when you don't want to give the person the chance to turn you down. They may still turn you down, but they have to call you and tell you. In the meantime, you can go on your merry way assuming you'll get the information eventually. Bizfolks refer to this with the crusty old tennis metaphor, "The ball's in your court."

Voice mail is also good if you want to avoid getting hung up with a chatterbox. Of course, both these strategies rely on calling when the person isn't in, so that their voice mail picks up.

Some people can get mean with voice mail. Here's a story from one office worker I'll call Tiffany:

> I was having a meeting in my office with another department head, Andy, with the door closed, basically trying to seek his advice on how to deal with my boss better. My boss walked by several times—I could see, because my office has a window. While

> I was in this meeting, I got a voice mail from my boss. I didn't see that I'd gotten it until after Andy had left. It said, "Tiffany, as of Monday I want you to let your assistant go. You said you were going to get me a report on why you need her and you haven't gotten it to me yet, and I don't see the productivity there. And if you're going to come into my office to discuss this you better have a very good plan. Don't say you just need her." I found that to be one of the most insulting things—to be told by voice mail to fire what I believed was a key position.

The plan, however, backfired. Tiffany grabbed Andy and went into her boss's office on another excuse and was able to buy a month's time.

Anytime you call somebody, be prepared to leave a voice mail message, even if you've got a long-winded explanation—*especially* if you've got a long-winded explanation. If you just hang up or say "Call me," the person has no idea what you want. They might even avoid you because they think you're calling about that five bucks you loaned them for lunch. If you tell them what you need, they can get it together before calling you back.

**E-Mail** If you've got e-mail in your office, count yourself lucky. Like a memo, you can compose a very careful message—even making it read like you just typed it in casually—but e-mail has more urgency.

It also gives you access to people whose attention you might not normally be able to get. Not long ago a writer for *The New Yorker* was doing a profile of Bill Gates, the head of Microsoft. He decided to send him an e-mail on CompuServe, just to see what would happen. After that, he went to the kitchen to feed the cat. When he came back, Bill had answered him.

You can do the same thing in your company, getting to the CEO if you need to. You can't be sure she'll answer you, but you can be reasonably sure she'll read it. Needless to say, something this powerful is also dangerous. Use with caution.

On a more everyday use, you can use e-mail as you would voice mail—sending info or requests to people you don't want to talk to. But unlike voice mail, you can pack a lot more stuff into e-mail: numbers, lists, addresses, etc. You can float an idea and include as much detail as a memo but make it seem more like a notion you had. You can work on it for days if you need to so you can get that just-right off-the-cuff feel. If the receiver hates your idea, he can tell you so and then banish it from his life with a keystroke. If you send a memo, there's the question of what to do with it. Write his response and send it back to you? Probably—and until he gets around to it, the piece of paper sits on his desk reminding him of what an idiot you are. You spent all this time writing and sending a memo, and now he has to spend all this time dealing with it. It's a psychological thing, but very real.

Another neat trick with e-mail is a variation on the cover-your-ass memo. In case you can't figure it out, a CYA memo just documents something that you might need later to prove that you did or didn't do something. The gist of it could be, for example, "As we agreed when we met on Monday, I'll be responsible for the croissants and orange juice at the upcoming press conference, and you'll be responsible for all media contact." This is something you might send to the guy you just *know* is going to screw up, and you don't want the finger pointed at you. You could send him a memo and send a copy to his boss and your boss—that's the time-honored way. It also sends a big flashing message to him that you're covering your hiney.

Here's where e-mail comes in. First, reduce that message down to a casual blurb: "Larry—I'm making arrangements for the refreshments for that press conference. Since you're handling the media, could you get me an estimate of how many people will be there? Thanks!" Then e-mail it to him and to his boss and your boss if you think you need the coverage. Poor Larry will probably think nothing of it, and after he reads it, will delete it from his files. *But you save yours.* Since the computer has dated it, you've got a lock on when you sent it to him. After the debacle happens and Larry starts whining that you were supposed to call the *Yucca Valley Gazette,* you produce the e-mail.

Of course, this can be pulled on you, so remember two things. First, don't put anything in e-mail that would be incriminating if somebody saved it and printed it out later. And second, keep an eye out for what seems like an innocuous e-mail to you. What does it imply? If it doesn't seem quite right, write a correction, send it off, and save both messages. And as a general warning, remember that everybody's e-mail can usually be read and saved by the folks in the computer department. If the boss wants them to get something out of your file, they'll do it.

Even if you don't feel the need to use these tricks when you first arrive, my advice is to compose all your messages off-line before you send them until you get comfortable enough to wing it. If you don't know how to do this, get a computer techie to show you. It's too often the case that when people don't know how to use the system they send a half-message, or a blank page, or a message they meant to revise. It makes you look like a dope. Get it right instead of sending something embarrassing into the void where the digerati can laugh at you.

**The Hard Stuff** As you've probably gathered from the discussion above, putting something on paper has a whole different psychological impact than sound bytes or screen blips. It's substance. It takes up space on a desk. It's a physical thing that has to be dealt with—this makes it seem somehow more real. I've told you why you might not want to put your ideas in this form, but other times this solidity is exactly what you want.

Printed words carry a long tradition of being "truer" than spoken words. When someone refers to a "published account" of something, the underlying assumption is that somebody made sure there was a factual basis to it—which of course, could be malarkey. But old habits die hard, and when people see something printed, they tend to believe it first and ask questions later. (And just as an aside, since word processors can use fonts that look exactly like the ones respectable publications use, the effect is further enhanced.) So—use paper when you want to have a stronger, more permanent effect, but realize that you'll be held to a higher standard of truth.

Putting something in writing lets you compose everything perfectly. Sometimes you have to do this so you can toss off more impressive facts that you have space for in an e-mail. Sometimes you'll want to use a more formal tone, one that would be out of place on the net.

Another reason for paper is to get your idea physically on the desk of the terminally busy or those with pathetically short attention spans. With these people you know you couldn't talk fast enough to get all the details out before they'd be checking their watches and fidgeting, and they might just blow off an e-mail.

Unlike the e-mail CYA trick above, you might want to document something on paper so everyone knows it's now on paper—and will be saved. I'll remind you one more time: the reverse of this is also important. Don't put anything on paper that you wouldn't want anyone else in the office to see. If you can, don't put anything on paper that you wouldn't be happy for *anyone*—including people outside the company—to see. Memos, reports, letters, and other hard copy are generally regarded as belonging to the company, not to you. That doesn't mean that the secretary is going to rifle through your files just to see what you've been up to, but even that can happen if you're out sick and your boss needs what you've got. If you want to bitch about what a jerk Cressfield is and want some advice about how to get him out of your face, don't commit that to paper—talk it out.

**Memos** Notice how I've got this separate section on memos, just as if it's a completely different medium of communication? Guess what? It is. Or maybe more like half a medium.

Memos have a cherished place in the hearts of bizfolks because the form is all theirs. Anybody can use the phone, write a letter, or leave a recorded message; even e-mail is used by every teen on the Internet. But memos—ah, it's a *business* thang.

The original idea behind memos was probably what we use e-mail for today—short, informal communication. Most memos are still that, but there's a lot more that can go on behind the scenes to make them *seem* casual when they are really a finely crafted cog in the cranking machinery of a political move. But I'll start with the basics.

Most memos are sort of like a formalized, perfectly articulated phone call. If your message is more complicated than that, maybe it should be a report. If it's less complicated, maybe it should be a phone call.

Don't use a memo to ask a simple question that can be answered on the phone or by e-mail. And don't write a memo just because someone asked you to—they may be up to no good. "That's a very interesting criticism you have about the Weenie Wrangler product line, Roger," your friendly coworker might say, and then, "Why don't you send me a memo on that." What they mean is, "I don't think I have enough rope to hang you with unless you send me some more." In that case you should demur, and say you still have some more thinking to do.

The more controversial the subject, the more important it is to have a conversation first and then put out a memo. It's especially tempting on touchy subjects to use e-mail or voice mail because less yelling is likely, but this chicken's way out can backfire when Mr. Thunderwhumpus becomes roaring mad instead of tickled pink at the bit of levity you thought would soften the blow. Better to face the onslaught.

Although there are millions of kinds of memos, there are some common species you might want to use:

- THE NOW WE UNDERSTAND EACH OTHER MEMO • This puts down in writing what you talked about so everybody has it straight. This can be manipulative, as I said before, but it can also be innocent and useful—just a master plan from which everyone can work.

- THE IT'S UNDER CONTROL MEMO • Here you tell people news about what you're doing or what you learned and let them know you're handling things. Get in the habit of sending these to your boss and she'll think you're very together.

- THE GOOD JOB MEMO • You can be a hero very easily by sending memos to people with whom you've worked on a project, saying what a great job they did. Send a copy to your boss and their boss, too. It's cheap and easy, and besides that, it's a *mitzvah*—a good deed your refined breeding obligates you to perform. Putting a compliment in writing is important because a copy goes in the person's file. You can also send out a "good job" memo about yourself under the guise of an It's Under Control memo. It tells the news, but it includes stuff that makes you look good.

- CYA • The legendary Cover Your Ass memo. You can use one of these to disagree with somebody ("I want to go on record as saying I think that chocolate-flavored burritos will never sell") or to lay blame where it's due. For example, if you think Bill in Receiving is nuts for swearing to you that the Nantucket Noodle Company can deliver ninety thousand noodles in nine days, there's no need to call Bill a liar. Just send him a memo that says you're relying on his word, and send a copy to your boss and his boss. The most important thing about a CYA memo is that you should save it.

• THE HOW ABOUT WE TRY THIS MEMO • Here's where you've got a half-baked idea and you want other people to help you. Sending out a memo like this lets people know your synapses are functioning. Typically, you ask for people's opinions. For a new kid especially, this is a great way to make an impression at work. When you're thinking, "Why the hell don't they just . . ." that's the time to pretend you're in charge and figure out what you would do. Once you have, put it in a memo and send it out. You can use e-mail if you like, but paper makes it more substantial.

• THE PITCH MEMO • This memo is different from the How About memo because it's a hard sell. This often goes out after you've gotten a good response from a How About memo or after you've lined up some supporters. You've got the facts, you've got the numbers, you know your case is bulletproof. Here's where you pitch it. This is the kind of memo you sweat over. Typically it goes out to a different audience—the higher-ups: those who can put it into action with a wave of their magic Monte Blancs.

**Ways to Write Memos** Who a memo is from, who it is to, and who is copied are absolutely crucial. There's more here than you think. For example, who is a memo from? Let's say you're the new kid in the purchasing department, and by talking to the others you've found out about the screwy way paper clips are purchased. They say they've tried to tell the boss, but he won't listen. They tell you that because you're the new kid and the boss loves you so far, he'll listen to anything you say. You volunteer to write a memo suggesting the new way to do things. Your boss will know it's not just from you, even if you're the only one who signs it (and you should be).

Or here's another situation. In one job I had, my boss and I agreed that we needed a lot more equipment to get a desktop publishing department up and running. She suggested I find out all the facts, put together a memo that proposed what we should do, send it to her, and copy the president—*but to let her read the draft before I send it*. The reason she wanted to read the draft is that the memo wasn't really for her benefit; it was for the president's. She and I worked on it together. We went through three or four drafts. When it was solid, I sent it to her and copied the president. That let her walk into his office and make the pitch that got his approval.

Another time I had to settle a dispute between two people: one was a project manager who worked for me; the other was the head of research, who didn't. The problem was that the project manager was flaunting statistics that made him look good, and the researcher said the numbers were crap. Everybody was beginning to look bad. I mediated between them, and when I got them to agree to a middle ground, I suggested we put out a joint memo to show our solidarity. I wrote it and got their approval. It went out with all three of our names as authors. What it said was less important than that we all said it together.

**Memo Mechanics** Some companies have preprinted memo forms, but a lot don't, especially now since you're probably printing memos out of a computer. Anyway, take a look at the sample on page 144.

When you're sending a memo to a lot of people, find out what order they should be in. Some companies have different traditions—alphabetical or in order of hierarchy are the most common. People can get upset if they feel they've been slighted, as Moe probably has in this example (he being, by all accounts, the head Stooge).

> Date: April 24, 1994
>
> To: Larry, Moe, and Curly Joe
>
> From: Groucho
>
> CC: Harpo, Chico, Gummo
>
> Re: Nyt, nyt, nyt
>
> What makes you guys think that's funny? That's not funny. Now, shooting an elephant in your pajamas is funny, especially if you don't know how the elephant got into your pajamas. Why, I oughta murdalize ya!

CC stands for carbon copies. Most people just put "Copies" there instead of "CC" now.

"Re" stands for "regarding." In other words, the subject of your memo. It's common now for people to put "Subject" instead of "Re."

Don't sign it at the bottom; it's not a letter. If you want to, you can put your handwritten initials next to your name at the top; the idea is that this shows it's not counterfeit.

**A Few Words for You Beginners** You may be hot to write your very first memo after reading all this, but slow down. You should wait and see how memos are used in your particular tribe. At some companies, memos are grave and serious things, and no one writes one unless it's a Big Deal. Even at places that aren't so extreme, you probably shouldn't send a memo to people outside your immediate working group unless your boss approves of it.

A good place to get into the memo action is to attach one to some regular report you're responsible for, as sort of a cover letter to your boss. You can use it to showcase a few of your brilliant (but small) suggestions for improving things.

## How to Sound Like a Smart Person

This isn't a book about business writing, but there are a few things I should point out because they go so totally against what you learned in college. Here they are:

**The Passive Voice** How many times did your English teacher crab at you for using the passive voice in your writing? You know, saying "The dog was shot," instead of saying "He shot the dog." Your prof said passive writing was dull. You can't tell who's performing the action. Well, he was right, and for most writing the passive voice is a real snooze. But in business you'll be using it a lot. And for exactly the reason your prof told you not to use it—because in a passive phrase, you can't tell who was responsible.

In business, after the dog is dead, it's often stupid to point out who shot it. "Although the Grimly account was lost, I believe we can do better when we try for the Smarmy Snacks account" sounds a lot better than "Although Bob lost the Grimly account . . ." Don't abandon the active voice; just know where to use it. As a general rule, if it's good, make it active; if it's bad, make it passive.

**I, We, and You** As a corollary to the passive thing, think carefully before you use these pronouns. In general, don't use "you" if the news is bad. Don't say, "You shot the dog," say "I was disappointed that . . ." and then tag on a passive phrase like "the dog was shot." Using the word "we" can help in a lot of situations. If the passive voice is just too wimpy for you to stand in certain situations, you can always say, "we really screwed up and I know we can do better." That way you share the responsibility. You can also use it to try to create teamwork where there might not really be much. Here's an example of moving from the specific I-you construction to the we construction: "If you can get me the information, I know we can get this project off the ground." In fact, the project may be entirely yours, but putting it this way can help create a team spirit.

**Clichés** Use 'em. Yes, I said use clichés—especially shopworn business talk like "get them on board" or "go the extra mile" or "join the team." In business, you're talking to all levels of people, all ages, all political persuasions. Clichés add informality without risk and a familiarity that's comforting to most people. And using business clichés shows you're part of the team. See, I slipped one in right there. Now don't lose your head and go hog-wild. That won't cut the mustard. Just one every once in a while will do.

**Break It Up** Try to write short—not more than two pages. If you can't write that short, use headings, subheadings, and bullets to cut it into chunks. Organize your memo in a way that someone who doesn't know the material can *see* how it's organized.

## Liar, Liar, Pants on Fire

Sooner or later, somebody in your company is going to ask you to lie. Yes, to fib, to distort, to stretch the truth, to fudge the data, to tweak the findings, to dazzle them with bullshit. Don't be alarmed. If your experience is typical, it won't be much different from the lying you've done your whole life ("Mom, I was at the library almost the whole time, I *swear*"). It'll just seem horrifying when you first do it. One manager I talked to remembers when she saw a young woman just out of school freak when she had to be creative with the data:

> We were working on a presentation that my boss was going to be giving on what the trends were nationally. It's one of those things that's very difficult to get statistics for. We had to show what was

> happening in our company's different markets. In all our markets, demand was going up, but in one state, the particular statistics we got said it was going down. We had no explanation for why it was going down. We asked Saskya to fudge the data. She was very uncomfortable with this—she was two weeks out of school. It was quoting from articles. It's not like she had done a survey. I would not feel comfortable asking somebody to fudge data of their own research. I'm sure that when I was twenty-two I would have been shocked to be told to ignore the fact that one state was going down. But now . . . it is an example of one of those things that changes.

That doesn't mean you bump up the profit figure in the annual report by a couple of mil. It just means that you shouldn't get too excited if you're asked to exaggerate a bit. You can figure out where your tolerance level is.

Chapter 7

# Smells Like Team Spirit: Corporate Culture

EVERY COMPANY, BIG OR SMALL, HAS A CORPORATE CULTURE. THAT IS, THE COLLECTION OF VALUES THAT THE COMPANY WANTS TO INSTILL IN ITS EMPLOYEES. DO YOU WANT TO ABSORB THESE VALUES? THAT WILL DEPEND ON WHAT YOU THINK OF THE VALUES THAT ARE COMMON TO ALMOST ALL CORPORATE CULTURES AND ON THE VALUES OF THE SPECIFIC ONE YOU'RE IN RIGHT NOW.

Back in Chapter 2, I delivered unto you The Four Harsh Realities of Planet Bizness. To refresh your memory, they are:

• THE CUSTOMER IS ALWAYS RIGHT •

• COMPANIES MUST MAKE MONEY •

• COMPANIES MUST EXPLOIT HUMAN TALENT, SKILL, AND LABOR TO MAKE MONEY •

• COMPANIES ARE ORGANIZED INTO HIERARCHIES •

All corporate cultures, those of the huge and those of the puny, are founded on the bedrock of these realities. We'll skip the first two. I pretty much covered these and the way they influence a company's values back in Chapter 3, *Clients and Other Money People*.

So let's start with what happens when companies exploit people to make money.

## A Short Course on Why Work Can Drive You Bonkers

You'll hear it soon enough. Jim, the guy in the next cube, will lean close with a smirk on his face, jerk his thumb over his shoulder to show you he's talking about poor old Oscar, and say, "Nice guy, but he can't sell worth a damn."

That short sentence sums up what one corporate view on how important it is to be nice might be. In this case, it's irrelevant. In general, any human quality that doesn't help the corporation is irrelevant. Oscar might spend his weekends slinging a ladle in a soup kitchen to help the homeless, but it means squat to the corporation. On the flip side, if Oscar was a mean son of a bitch but could sell everybody else under the table, then that would be fine.

Or, if Oscar was a real sweetheart and that caused all his customers to buy from him year after year, then the company would not only encourage his sweetness but would try to get the whole sales staff to be nice like Oscar. In that case the company would fire any sons of bitches on the staff it could find.

What a corporation does, then, to exploit your talent, skill, and labor, is to sift through your qualities, encourage the ones that help it, ignore the ones that don't, and squash the ones that hurt it.

It's not that the corporation is evil. It's just amoral. Nothing personal, bub. However, the human psyche responds rather poorly to this treatment. This is a big pain to the corporation and can be less than pleasant for you.

Here's how psychiatrist Douglas LaBier describes it in his book *Modern Madness* (Simon & Schuster/Touchstone):

> An internal selection process occurs in which personal traits and attitudes that are most useful to the work and the roles at any given level get supported and reinforced. Those that are not as useful, or which are unnecessary, are discouraged, thwarted, unused, and are gradually weakened. So the result is a selection and gradual molding of certain kinds of orientations for different kinds of work, a congruent fit between what is required by the work and the character of those who do the work.

So one function of corporate culture is to take you apart and put you back together the way it likes you.

The corporate culture in any company is going to mold you. The trick is to try to keep an eye on yourself to see if you like what it's encouraging—and if you're happy to get rid of what it's discouraging in you. Ask yourself: Would you like you if you met you after having worked for this company for five years?

This is probably a good place to point out the difference between what goes on at work that is part of the corporate culture and what is just part of the human landscape, because it's sometimes easy to mistake one for the other. Corporate culture is made up of values that are important to the corporation, qualities in people that help it serve customers and make money. People come and go, but the values stay.

Now there is another set of values that individuals bring in, and if that person is your boss, you might mistake these values as part of the corporate culture. Here's an example of what one worker told me:

> My boss would hire these women, and their personal stuff was very important to her. Although she was a very successful career woman, she was also very into what I perceive as the very frilly, feminine things. China was just so important to her; what people's china patterns were, what their silver patterns were.

This boss reinforced the value of status as defined by your china pattern. If you wanted to get along with her, you better care about china. *But this has nothing to with corporate culture.* The corporation could give a flying Frisbee about china. When this boss leaves the corporation, so will the value, unless her underlings stick around and decide to carry on the grand tradition.

The reason to stay clear about this is so you don't pin your hopes on fitting in with some weird quirk your boss has. Otherwise you might miss the big picture, get fired, and be shouting down the hall as the security guards drag you away, *"But I have the right china!"*

There will also be values that seem like weird quirks yet are part of the corporate culture. They won't usually be tied to anyone in particular, except maybe the founder of the company. Whatever these values are, the corporation as a whole has either found that they work or believes that they work to help make money. Some companies insist that their male employees have short hair. Whether this really helps make money for the company is debatable, but at some time in the company's history enough people in the company believed in this so that it became part of the corporate culture.

Sometimes the weird values that a company has can be incredibly humanitarian—and profitable at the same time. At Ben & Jerry's ice cream, for example, the founders practically *demand* that everybody who works there thinks about social responsibility. They buy ingredients, like blueberries, from the Passamaquoddy Indians and brownies from a company that uses profits to house the homeless. They offer employees fantastic benefits: health care is completely free, dependents (including gay partners and unmarried heterosexual partners) are covered for only 10 percent of the premium, on-site child care is provided, and runaway executive salaries are kept in check by a rule that says no one can make more than seven times what the lowest-paid worker makes (this may change when a new CEO comes on). The company even has a position called director of social mission development. Does all this sell ice cream? All I know is I'll buy a Peace Pop before a candy bar any day, knowing that my money goes to an enlightened company and a good cause.

Then there's Patagonia, a company that makes clothing and outdoor equipment, which was founded by a rock-climber who thinks people work too much. He only works half a year, and a lot of his employees surf for a few hours over lunch or take off months at a time to trek up some glacier. At Tandem Computers, the founder hates structure and is big on thinking about alternatives—hence, Tandem has a philosophy department, where they work on their culture's fundamental beliefs and values. The president at Marquette Electronics says this in the employee handbook: "There are no time clocks because we assume you're honest. When you want to call home you don't have to use a pay phone; there are phones everywhere for local calls. We don't tell you what to wear, we just want you to do a good job. . . . We strive to avoid hierarchy and organization charts, although, obviously, there has to be some chain of command. But if you want to talk to me or any other 'boss' feel free to do so."

In companies like these, there's little difference between the company's values and the founder's values—and as you can see, that can be a pretty good deal. If you're fortunate enough to find a place like this (you lucky dog), don't be afraid to pin your hopes on these values—they're probably a permanent part of the company's landscape.

## I'm Better Than You Because It Says So Right Here

Now we'll look at Harsh Reality Number Four, that all organizations are hierarchies. Among the jillions of ways humans can organize their relations with each other—as a family, a tribe, a kibbutz, a poker game, a utopian society, a soccer team, a rock band, a street gang—corporate hierarchies, especially big fat honking ones, have lovable traits all their own.

The first thing to notice about a hierarchy is that according to its rules, *positions* have power—not people. That is, your boss can tell you what to do because she holds the position of being your boss. If she gets fired tomorrow, you don't have to do what she says. You have to obey the person that gets her old position.

Like a lot of things in business, this is weird and not the normal way of our species. Normally you'd do what somebody says because they have some *personal* power. You do what a mechanic says because the mechanic has the know-how to fix your car and you don't. You don't obey him because he holds a position of authority over you. With luck, your boss does have some skill, knowledge, or talent that you think is worth offering your allegiance to, and according to the rules of the hierarchy, this must be so or your boss would never have been put in that position.

But we know this isn't necessarily so. Your boss might command precisely zero of your respect. In her book *Beyond Power* (Ballantine), Marilyn French explains what hierarchies do to handle the situation when you have to obey someone you think has no business telling you what to do: "Because of this contradiction—and examples of it are rife in any structure of any size—all hierarchies operate by coercion. They must coerce a complaisance they cannot earn." French makes clear what that coercion can be:

> Coercion varies in kind and degree. In some structures the threat may be a bad report, no raise this year, dismissal. . . . In its subtler forms it may be a weak smile informing you of the displeasure of someone whose respect you value, or sighs, or raised eyebrows, all of which are really warnings. . . . Whatever its forms, techniques of coercion essentially threaten expulsion from the institution . . . . *Every hierarchy maintains itself by the inculcation of fear.*

But most organizations don't like to blatantly use fear unless they have to. "Fear [is] perhaps the most effective motivator yet discovered for the short term," says Stanley Bing in *Crazy Bosses* (Pocket Books), "but it generates a kind of obedience that is difficult to maintain over time." Another problem with fear is it smashes ideas, as Alvin Toffler says in *Powershift* (Bantam), "Fear is the primary idea-assassin. Fear of ridicule, punishment, or loss of job destroys innovation."

So hierarchies don't rely on fear exclusively but use reward as well. The reward you get is to move up in the hierarchy. That means you usually get more money. You also have a better chance to get your ideas put into action because you can call the shots by the authority of your position, not of your ideas. You don't have to go around convincing everyone how brilliant your scheme is—which would be a demonstration of personal power. Instead, you can just decree that your scheme is what everybody will do—which is an example of hierarchical power.

Hierarchical power is good in that it can get things done over the objections of dimwits who don't have the vision to see what should be done, but it's bad in that stupid ideas can be launched in spite of the warnings of brilliant underlings.

## Life on the Ladder

Seems pretty straightforward, doesn't it? People in hierarchies are motivated by fear on one hand and reward on the other. And, these two values being common to all hierarchies, they form the bedrock for all corporate cultures. Ah, but like any neat cause-and-effect system, once it's up and running it starts developing its own, totally unexpected values—sort of side effects. Probably the most important were discovered by a guy named Dr. Laurence J. Peter. His main idea is called the *Peter Principle* (detailed in the book *The Peter Principle,* by Peter and Raymond Hull, Bantam), and it goes like this:

> In a hierarchy every employee tends to rise to his level of incompetence.

This happens because as long as people do a good job where they are, they're eligible for promotion. When they get to a position where they can only do a mediocre job, they're not eligible for promotion. And that's where they stay.

Maybe you've never heard of this before, or maybe you've heard it so much it seems trite and not worth considering. But Peter's insight actually leads to some rather scary ideas about hierarchies, which I see as the following five truisms:

**There Are Probably Lots of Incompetent People Where You Work** The longer the average length of time people have been around in your company, the more likely it is that they've risen to their incompetence level. Peter's Corollary states, "In time, every post tends to be occupied by an employee who is incompetent to carry out its duties." That doesn't mean that people with a lot of seniority are stupid, or that their experience means nothing, or that they can't be helpful and amaze you with what they know. It just means that in spite of all this, they may be very bad at their jobs.

**It's the New People Who Get Things Done** Peter points out that "Work is accomplished by those employees who have not yet reached their level of incompetence." Often, when a company becomes immobilized by incompetence, it will add positions to the hierarchy. This works for a while until the new hires are promoted to their level of incompetence.

**A Lot of Good People Will Leave** Peter calls this "summit competence." This happens when someone is still good at a job but can't be promoted because there's nowhere to go. In that case, the person moves on to another company and another job, usually mumbling something about "a greater challenge" on the way out. Eventually these people find their level of incompetence elsewhere.

**A Lot of Good People Will Get Bad Reviews** That's because incompetent people will be reviewing them. Peter says that if a boss is still competent, he'll evaluate his staff on the real work they do; stuff that accomplishes something in the world outside the company. If a boss has risen to his incompetence level (as they all do, sooner or later, according to the theory) then he will evaluate his staff on how well they pick nits—follow rules, fill out forms, kiss butt.

You might be doing a great job at servicing customers, but because you're not filling out form 483749-FKR-857EJD-87R949348 correctly you get a black mark on your record.

**A Lot of Good People Will Get Fired** Specifically, these will be people who are *too* good at their jobs. They'll get the boot because the underlying supposition in a hierarchy is that people at a particular level do work appropriate to that level. If you do work way above your level, it causes three problems. First, it makes everybody else on your level look bad, and that wrecks morale. Second, it makes your boss look bad—why hasn't she been able to accomplish what you are now doing? Third, it makes the organization look bad—here's someone who's come in and proved that the organization's hierarchy is inefficient by easily accomplishing more than what the hierarchy says should be possible on that level.

Besides the Peter Principle, there's another famous rule that's been made about how hierarchies work. Discovered by C. Northcote Parkinson, it's called Parkinson's Law (from his book, *Parkinson's Law,* Ballantine), and it declares:

> Work expands so as to fill the time available for its completion.

Parkinson says the law comes from two observations:

> (1) "An official wants to multiply subordinates, not rivals" and (2) "Officials make work for each other."

He shows what happens when an official, whom he calls A, feels overworked: The official, A, won't ask for somebody to be hired at his own level to help him because that would bring in someone who might get promoted instead of him. Instead, he asks for subordinates, C and D, which gives A more status. Eventually C will ask for subordinates, and so on, until there's a gob of people doing a gob of meaningless work:

> An incoming document may well come before each of them in turn. Official E decides that it falls within the province of F, who places a draft reply before C, who amends it drastically before consulting D, who asks G to deal with it. But G goes on

> leave at this point, handing the file over to H, who drafts a minute that is signed by D and returned to C, who revises his draft accordingly and lays the new version before A. . . . He reads through the draft with care, deletes the fussy paragraphs added by C and H, and restores the thing back to the form preferred in the first instance by the able (if quarrelsome) F. He corrects the English—none of these young men can write grammatically—and finally produces the same reply he would have written if officials C to H had never been born. Far more people have taken far longer to produce the same result. No one has been idle. All have done their best.

You won't have to spend much time in the Halls of Hierarchy to see this happen in real life. The larger the company, the more likely this is to happen, and with any kind of government job, it's just about a certainty because in government there's no natural limit—like the need to make a profit—to stop people from asking for more positions all the way up the line.

I was once hired as a payroll clerk in city government. It was a new position requested by my supervisor. I was her only underling. After I was there a few months, it dawned on me that she no longer had anything to do except make sure I was making the appropriate little marks in the appropriate little boxes. She reviewed my work—that was her job.

## I Guess You Are the Boss of Me

One of the strange things about a hierarchy is that you can't seem to turn its power off. Theoretically, when you're not at work or doing things that don't relate to work your boss shouldn't be able to tell you what to do. But it's easy to get locked into thinking that somebody who's your superior at work is your superior, period. And some bosses like it that way. One worker tells of the time her boss pulled rank outside the office:

> Once she was giving an engagement party for a woman who worked for me. I had a fever, and I didn't feel well. She was giving a formal party. I called her up Saturday morning and said, "I've got a fever. I've got to stay in bed." She said, "Come." Like an edict. She *commanded* me to come. So I went and helped.

When he worked on Wall Street, Ed Seider also got a good look at hierarchy enforced through social conventions. In the break room there was a table where Those of Large Importance took their espresso and croissants. One did not sit one's butt at the table if one knew what was good for one. Although Ed thought he had a pretty friendly relationship with his boss, he found out that there were limits. His boss would boast about his prowess on the squash court, so one day Ed challenged him, in a friendly way, saying "When am I going to see how good you are on the squash court? Let's play after work." His boss said, "I don't think so," in a way that obviously meant, "Don't ask me again. It isn't going to happen."

## The King Is Dead! Or At Least He Feels Really Bad

All of the above pretty much sums up the bad news about hierarchies, which underlie all companies and all corporate culture. The good news is that the hierarchical structure has been dying for years. "Hardly a day passes without some new article, book, or speech decrying the old top-down forms of pyramidal power," says Alvin Toffler in *Powershift*. The reasons for dumping the old power pyramid include those above, and some new ones brought about by the much feared and talked-about Age of Information.

In the old days, hierarchies could be stable. The boss typically knew more than those he supervised because the body of information he had to learn stood relatively still. When he learned it, he became wise, and so his place in the hierarchy could be based not just on his position of authority but on his personal power: his wisdom.

But now, everything's going so fast, it is not just common, but typical, that you know more than your boss. You're out there up to your waist in the information stream, catching everything that goes by. Your boss can only shout from the shore, "What'd ya catch?"

This doesn't just threaten the authority of your boss; this threatens the whole idea of why the hierarchy is built the way it is. Alvin Toffler says, "Put most briefly, the way we organize knowledge frequently determines the way we organize people—and vice versa. When knowledge was conceived of as specialized and hierarchical, businesses were designed to be specialized and hierarchical." But knowledge ain't in neat little packages anymore. The Information Age, Toffler points out in *Powershift,* is making hierarchies explode like a school of bloated fish:

> In short, the cubbyhole scheme designed for Year One becomes inappropriate for Year Two. It is easy to reclassify or sort information stored in a computer. Just copy a file into a new directory. But try to change organizational cubbyholes! Since people and budgets reflect the scheme, any attempt to redesign the structure triggers explosive power struggles. The faster things change in the outside world, therefore, the greater the stress placed on bureaucracy's underlying framework and the more friction and infighting.

Faced with what lots of people see as the general failure of hierarchies to get off their butts and do something, some innovators in corporate America have started tinkering—did I say tinkering? Make that *dismantling*—the lumbering machine of bureaucracy.

Take Bob Gore, for example. His dad founded W. L. Gore & Associates in 1958 on his own management theory, which he called a "lattice organization." Bob still runs the company that way today, making stuff like Gore-tex (that breathable fabric they use in outdoor gear). So what is a lattice organization? Well, it's sort of nonorganization. Nobody has a title. Nobody has a boss. Everybody just does something they think is useful. They gather into teams and natural leaders emerge. Nobody can tell anybody else what to do—you have to convince your coworkers to join you in a project. They figure out compensation through a system of "sponsors" who help evaluate performance. Unbelievable as it may sound, this is how they run a company that has more than 5,000 employees in 40 plants all over the world and that makes more than $600 million a year.

At Cray Computers, unlike most places, you don't have to become a manager to move up the ranks—they've got a parallel track where technical and professional folk can get titles and bucks just for getting better at what they do. Even IBM is splitting itself into 14 different units, hoping to whittle down the bureaucratic monster and encourage teams.

So the old hierarchy is feeling poorly even in the hallowed halls of IBM. The question to you, though, is How's it doing where you live?

Let's take a moment to take your hierarchy's temperature. If you're lucky, it's got a high fever and is about to keel over. Here are the symptoms:

**Blocked Arteries** In a healthy hierarchy, everything is supposed to go through the "proper channels." If you have an idea or complaint, you're supposed to tell your boss and no one else. If you notice that people routinely ignore the channels and work with whoever they think can help, then the hierarchy has a case of poor circulation. But what's bad for the bureaucratic body is good for the germs trying to stir things up.

**Mutating Cells** People guard their domains vigorously—and are able to—in a strapping, strong hierarchy. They're very concerned with their titles and what their job description says they're in charge of. Like a white corpuscle on the rampage, they'll attack any foreign idea that threatens to infect their area—whether it's good or not. (This is known as the NIH syndrome. Ideas aren't accepted because they're "Not Invented Here.")

In cultures like this, organisms in different realms are seen as different beings, and it's unnatural for one to mutate into something else. When it happens, it's worthy of comment, as I had one worker point out:

> My boss had a habit of grooming young inexperienced women who might have been bright women but who had been in secretarial positions. That gave her a base of people whom she felt she had tremendous control over. But they didn't have the respect externally that she needed for her department to be perceived as real. One of these secretarial types has now been promoted up to assistant vice president. Not to undermine what that woman has done, but it took a long time for her to be perceived as having real authority.

But when a hierarchy weakens, the cell walls become permeable. People from different departments get together to work on projects. Ideas flow without restriction, and nobody worries much that it's a guy in accounting who's coming up with the good marketing ideas. When that happens, the whole physiology of the organization can begin to change.

**Parasitic Infection** Healthy hierarchies are supposed to use authority to enforce the will of the company. If bosses don't have to throw their weight around to get their employees to do what they think best, then the hierarchy is becoming irrelevant. These bosses are slowly killing the hierarchy because employees will come to expect that you do what your boss says because she knows what she's doing, not because she's your boss. If a supervisor gets hired who tries to enforce obedience through power only, there will be a revolt, and the hierarchy will be revealed for the sick creature it is.

**Rashes** Check the armpits of a healthy-looking hierarchy and you're liable to find something breaking out. It might be a small department that acts like a group of peers, ignoring the official status of its members. It might be a bunch of people from different departments who meet informally to work on a pet project. It's in these pockets that antihierarchical values grow and spread, usually because they just plain work better for the groups that are using them. If you can find some hotbeds of bureaucracy busters you might be able to join them or at least talk to one of their members long enough to see if you can't use some of their methods to form your own infectious breeding ground.

If you find signs that the hierarchy you're in is ailing, that's all the better for your health. If none of these signs are present, see if you can start an infection.

## And From the Folks Who Brought You Leave It to Beaver and Häagen-Dazs . . .

On top of the general nature of hierarchies, you've also got the influence of the gang of folks who've been laboring over the last few decades to keep these values a'goin'. They consist of two generations: the Silent Generation and the Boomers.

The Silents had a big dose of instability when they were growing up, going from the Depression straight into World War II. By the time the 1950s rolled around, they *liked* the idea of structure, conformity, and calm. To them, hierarchies seem like the obvious and natural way things should be. In 1957, William Whyte wrote an influential book called *The Organization Man* (Doubleday/Anchor), in which he described them as "a generation of bureaucrats." He goes on:

> Although they cannot bring themselves to use the word bureaucrat, the approved term—the "administrator"—is not significantly different in its implications. The man of the future, as junior executives see him, is not the individual but the man who works through others for others. . . . Where the immersion of the individual used to be cause for grumbling and a feeling of independence lost, the organization man of today is now welcoming it. He is not attempting to reverse the trend and to cut down the deference paid to the group; he is working to increase it, and with the help of some branches of the social sciences he is erecting what is almost a secular religion.

The super big shots in your organization—the CEO, the trustees, the board members, maybe even a lot of the vice presidents—are likely to be of this generation. The more of this generation who are in your company, the more its corporate culture will be structured, hierarchical, and group-oriented.

Next we have the Boomers—and you know their story. They wanted a better government and a better society; they settled for better ice cream. They grew up in the instability of Viet Nam protests, the sexual revolution, and the drug culture. The difference between them and the Silents is that they *liked* their instability, although they got sick of it eventually, too.

When they got down to business, they wanted that to be better, too. So they networked, dressed for success, bought beamers and cellular phones and now worry about burnout. Most of them bought the hierarchical values, but because they still have a soft spot for revolutionary ideas and still think of themselves as being the new breed, they're often the ones reading all those books about how to junk the old system.

Sometimes members of this generation will pretend like the hierarchy has already been junked. They'll be all egalitarian until you do something they don't like and then they'll pull rank. In general, they're schizo about their positions of power. They've got 'em, but they don't like to flaunt 'em. The more Boomers that are in your company, the more schizo its culture is likely to be.

Boomers are also big on commitment. They were committed to The Movement (any movement), committed to maximizing their personal growth, and so it was natural that they became committed to their jobs, like selling junk bonds was some kind of spiritual quest. That's what has made some of them workdogs. If you want to go home at five like your job description says, you may, oddly, get more support from the Silents who like rules than Boomers who think you should live and breath your commitment to your career.

## The Far-Flung Poles of Corporate Culture

So far I've just described the forces that have shaped all American corporate cultures, whether you're talking about IBM or Ricky's Quality Stove Liners, Inc. Now we turn our attention to four scales that famous scientists use to measure the differences among corporate cultures. (All the scientists are from tiny little countries you've never heard of so don't bother trying to find out about them.)

Keep in mind that if you're in a big corporation, you're surrounded by layers of corporate culture. You might be in a pocket of democracy while a fascist dictatorship rages outside. Or it might be the other way around. Part of this depends on your boss, part on the general culture of the company, and part on the kind of work that you do. People in the graphics department, for example, are allowed to be a little flaky. That's part of the universally recognized culture of artistic types.

There isn't really such a thing as a good or bad corporate culture, except from your point of view. What I try to do here is to let you know what kind of cultures are out there so you get a picture of how yours stacks up.

Obviously, there are as many different corporate cultures as there are businesses. But just as they all have hierarchical values in common to a greater or lesser degree, their other values tend to revolve around the yin and yang of a few other poles. Here are the ones I've been able to discover:

**Einstein vs. Picasso** A lot of corporate culture—and a lot of clashes between corporate cultures—can be explained with this polarity: the familiar science/art duality. It's the number-crunchers against the word crafters, the propeller heads against the creative flakes, the crew in research against the crew in marketing. Typically, each thinks the other is insane.

You're in a heavily science culture if everything has to be quantified, especially things like goals and projections. You're in an art culture if you've got to qualify everything. More than some of the other value polarities here, the Science vs. Art polarity is one that you have to figure out department by department. A company's overall culture may be one or the other, but they're bound to have some departments that are different.

The strange thing about these cultures is that each one wants to be the other. The researchers want you to think what they do is an art. The crew in public relations wants you to know everything they do is very scientific. Once you've determined that the culture you're in leans one way, the secret to impressing people is to convince them that you've got a strong talent for the other side. You've got to satisfy the minimum requirements of your culture, but then you're free to show your multicultural side.

For example, let's say your job is to keep track of the monthly sales figures—a scientific job on the face of it. You can score extra points by analyzing what you think the figures mean. You're putting values (assigning qualities) to raw data and making judgments and projections—this is art.

If you've been hired to write for the company newsletter, see if you can't attach some numbers to what you do. Maybe you can find studies that show that seventy-five percent of a typical company's employees aren't aware of all their employee benefits. That's a scientific approach to pitching your idea about writing an article on the company's benefits.

Of course the science/art polarity isn't just in business. It's through our whole society, and if you're pegged on one side or the other, you're assumed to have certain characteristics.

Aside from your work, don't let the culture you're in define you. If you're in the accounting department, let people know you can read more than digits. If you're in art, take an interest in statistics.

**Do It Now vs. Do It Right** There's an idea in business that there are three factors to any job: time, money, and quality. The expression that covers it is this: Tell me what two of them have to be and I'll tell you what the third one will be. So, for example, if your boss wants something of high quality but there's little money, then you'll need time to figure out how to do it. If you don't have time or money, then the quality is going to be crappy. If the quality has to be high but you don't have much time, then you'll have to spend a lot of money to get it done.

Although business types love this idea, they almost never go by it, especially when they give you instructions. They want everything fast, cheap, and right. And from the view of the general worker, this often gets boiled down to the conflict between speed and care, because the money issue has already been defined higher up in the company.

Although the corporate cultures of most companies fall somewhere between the pace of the Baja 100 and the safety of a school bus, looking at these extremes will help you get a fix on how fast and carefully your company drives.

Corporate cultures running at the maximum clock rate often have these characteristics: They're younger companies, often with the owner or founder cranking as if it's the last day to make money; they're dictatorial (although that doesn't mean the hierarchy is necessarily strong—sometimes you've just got a houseful of bullies all fighting each other); they're entrepreneurial; they have few defined procedures (nobody knows what they're doing until they do it) and work tends to get reworked over and over and over again. I've worked in a few of these joints. In one, I was fired because I insisted on taking a day off—a day I had gotten approval for long in advance. The day after the holiday the owner called me and asked if I would come back to work. Getting stuff out the door fast was so important to her she didn't care if she had to break her original promise to give me a day off or if she had to take back her threat to fire me. I saw the same thing happen to someone else in another speed factory.

When you're running as fast as you can, you don't have time to think about where you're going. Someone I'll call Roberto told me that if anyone in his office stopped long enough to consider what they should do, the boss called that "process" and wouldn't stand for it:

> The biggest difference between the president of the company and me is that he considers process a four-letter word. And he says it as such. "Oh, that's *process*. Yuck." He threatened me. Somebody had

> gotten fired at a sister company, and he said, "She got fired because she was into *process,* not sales." He has no respect for analysis. He's quick to point fingers if something goes wrong, but [in spite of this] thinks things should just happen.

On the other end of the spectrum are those places that believe it's better to be safe than sorry, and they are *never, ever* sorry. These places tend to be bigger, older companies with complicated hierarchies, lots of procedures, and lots of paperwork. The emphasis is on approval. Everything has to be approved, mulled over. Everything has to go through the right channels. If you can die of a heart attack working for the speed junkie described above, you can turn into a chunk of petrified wood in a place like this.

In Do It Now cultures people usually get promoted because they work long, frenetic hours and always push (sometimes recklessly) to get things done. If you can take the heat, you not only get to stay in the kitchen—they put you right into the frying pan.

In Do It Right cultures, the people that rise are the meticulous, consistent workers. Hillary Jacobs, who worked for a phone company, said that most of the people in top management started out as pole-climbers who played it safe for twenty or thirty years. These cultures are sometimes so afraid of speed that someone standing still can survive, as Hillary notes:

> I had a person who was referred to as a *put.* A put is anybody who was put in your department because of that person's connection with someone higher up in the company. This guy was not interested in working at all, and he was protected in some way. He used to come to meetings without a pencil. He would play video games at his desk shamelessly. And he would steal chairs out of my

> office. And there wasn't a whole lot I could do about it.

This could not happen in a Do It Now culture. Other kinds of incompetence can, usually in the form of someone who botches a job seven or eight times before they get it right because they're trying to move at warp speed.

There's not a lot you can do to fight your company's culture on the speed spectrum. If you're stuck in a company at one of the extremes, the important thing to know is that other ways of working do exist. When you look for a new job, don't work for a small, young company if you hate speed, and don't work for the government if you hate systems and approvals.

**By the Book vs. By the Seat of Your Pants** We're talking regulations here. Fussiness over regulations often correlates with the speed/care factor just described. That is, quick companies don't worry about regs; big, slow ones do.

But this isn't always true, because the regulations can often come from outside the company. Take the case of an advertising agency that gets the job of advertising the statewide lottery. Most ad agencies, by their nature, are pretty crazed with speed. But one that wins this account will have to slow down to make sure it meets the state's requirements. The agency's staff will have to show that they don't discriminate against women or minorities. They'll have to show that of the vendors they hire, a certain minimum percentage are women-owned or minority-owned. They'll have to produce advertising in all the languages required by state law. They'll have to submit detailed, long-range plans for approval—and stick to them, or else. And just because they've got the contract doesn't mean they've got the money. A government office can be incredibly slow at paying the bills because of all the regulations on the spending of public funds. The people in the advertising agency working on this account, then, will have to adapt themselves to an entirely different culture.

There are also big companies that don't move too fast but that aren't subject to much regulation. Let's say a company makes computer hard disks. They have to put a few warnings in the manual so users don't electrocute themselves, but besides that, they're pretty much regulation-free.

If you're in a culture that's regulation oriented, you've got to realize that they aren't kidding around. These are laws, and people get arrested if they misrepresent something on a report. Living in a regulated culture can be stultifying, but sometimes it feels better than working in a place where the boss always hires his disgusting brother-in-law's company as a vendor and there's nothing you can do about it.

**All for One vs. Leave Me Alone, Will You** Standardize or individualize? In business lingo this is known as centralizing or decentralizing. The question always is, how much independence should the separate parts of a company have (whether those parts are people or departments)? Independence gives greater freedom at the expense of control. Unlike the other culture polarities, any given company is usually going from one pole to the other and will probably reverse directions later on in its life.

Here's an example of what this looks like. Dwane, an influential v.p., is sick of sending his copies to the company's Department of Copying Services. It takes forever. The copies come back screwed up. He'd like to make his own copies, but corporate procedures prohibit it. So he stands up and says, "Hey! I know what's wrong! Our company's emphasis on control is strangling us. We need to get rid of that expensive tub of a copy machine, the Miracle 8000, and let each department get its own copier. We can save money by firing the staff in the Department of Copying Services and we'll be able to get our copies faster."

So they do, and everything works fine for a while. Dwane leaves the company, and Susumo replaces him. Soon Susumo is bugged because he notices that there is a copy machine every five feet down the hallway, and they're all different brands. Each department has its own service contract on its own machine, costing the company a fortune. Departments that don't have their own machine are agitating to get one, and in the meantime are paying other departments through a time-wasting interdepartmental charging system to get their copies made. So Susumo says, "Hey! I know what's wrong! We've got no control over what all the different departments are doing. We're duplicating efforts. If we pool our budgets and workload we can get the Miracle 8000 copy machine, hire a staff to run it, and do everything faster, cheaper, and better."

The same principle can apply to all kinds of issues. Should the sales staff work on individual commissions, which encourages independence but creates rivalries, or should it pool its commissions, which helps cooperation but might reduce ambition?

Typically, younger, smaller, and faster companies are less centralized; older, bigger, and slower ones more so. Most companies are more one than the other, but the wind can be blowing either way. It might be a steady breeze toward centralization in an already centralized administration or a hurricane blast of decentralization blowing like a blizzard through the redwoods, leaving the old-timers feeling naked and chilly.

Once you've gauged the direction and velocity, you can decide what you'll do. If there's a hurricane out there, don't try to fight it; it was probably started by the top blowhard. If it's not much more than a gust, you might get points by suggesting a little more of whatever the company doesn't have.

## Swell Number Magic

Here's a way you can estimate the four qualities above and combine them into a handy Corporate Culture Rating. First, get a pencil and some scratch paper. Now assign a scale of 1 to 13 1/2 for each of the four qualities. Pick a number that represents the strength of that quality. You can go over 13 1/2 or under 1 if you want to. Add them all together, divide by the number of days you've been working at the company, then add your telephone number and subtract your age. Got it? Good. You can save this number if you like, although I don't know why you would.

I've included this little exercise here to once again remind you that *no matter what I or anybody else says, people and their ways of interacting are basically mysteries.* Who knows? You may be working in a completely alien kind of company, unknown until this very moment. You are free to raise your hand at any moment and say, "Excuse me. Mr. Soden? Uh, you're full of it, sir."

# PART 3

# Where You're Supposed to Get To

Chapter 8

# Who's Got the Power

ALL RIGHT, ALL YOU POWER-MAD DEMONS. YOU'VE LOST ALL PATIENCE HEARING ME PRATTLE ON ABOUT HIERARCHIES AND HOW DESTRUCTIVE THEY ARE TO THE HUMAN SPIRIT, AND ALL THAT OTHER WIMPY TALK ABOUT CORPORATE CULTURE AND ITS EFFECT ON THE FRAIL HUMAN EGO. WHAT YOU WANT TO KNOW IS HOW TO TELL WHO HAS MUSCLE WHERE YOU ARE AND HOW TO GET A LITTLE YOURSELF. FAIR ENOUGH.

In that case, it's back to the hierarchy, the foundation of all power in most organizations. The Official Hierarchy is contained in the organizational chart—that diagram with boxes and lines that tells who bosses who and who is the czar of what info. If your organization doesn't have one, it's worthwhile to make up your own.

On the face of it, a chart like this seems pretty clear. You can tell who has power in relation to someone else according to how high up they are on the chart. You can tell what they're in charge of because it says so in the box: Director of Client Services, for example. All this is well and good—you should assume that the chart is accurate until you know otherwise—but there are ways to learn more by studying the chart. Here's what to look for:

**The Drone Count** In general, the bigger the department, the more influential the top person of that department, even if her title is the same as someone with a smaller department. For example, the vice president in charge of marketing may have twice the staff as the vice president for research and development. Don't take size as an absolute, however. Someone who's in charge of a lot of worker bees is going to have less pull than someone who manages three directors.

Sometimes you'll find people who are called managers, but they don't have any staff at all. This might be because their staff was swept out from under them (see the second case under "Ambiguous Titles" below) or it may be because their supervisor has enough clout to get his underlings up to the manager's level even though they don't manage anyone.

**The Food Chain** Near the bottom, you might have two supervisors with the same title, same number of workers, similar kind of work. To see if one has an edge, follow the chain of command up to see where it tops out. You might find that one's ultimate boss is the head of accounting, somebody no one listens to, whereas the other's boss o' bosses is Sandra Who Walks on Water. It's likely that the person in Sandra's food chain has more pull.

**Money Departments** Money equals power. The way this works in organizations is that the departments that have bigger roles in the money-making function of the company have more power. Which may not be as obvious as you might think. For example, in a company that's made ball bearings for a million years, the sales department might have the clout, whereas at Blammo Whammo Games their fortunes may rest on the gang of gleebs in game development. Managers and executives in departments that are just part of normal business (personnel, accounting, etc.), often have less power.

**The Secretaries** The hierarchy of secretaries forms a parallel universe to the power of the people they serve. And the physical laws of that universe spill right over into the main one all the time. It's not just that secretaries who serve more powerful people are higher up than the secretaries who serve less powerful people. A big shot's secretary is often more powerful than a floor full of junior-level assistants—especially if the secretary's been around for a while. These people are relied upon by their bosses for their good judgment as well as their skills. So look carefully at the chart and note the secretaries of the powerfolk. And act accordingly.

**Ambiguous Titles** Find a vague title, and you've found a power secret—either somebody with a lot of power or very little. The reason it's usually one or the other is that an ambiguous title is created so the person in that position won't be tied down.

Let's say that Jenny at National Thread and Thimble is great at selling clients *and* at writing company brochures. So they make her Director of Client Communication so she can do both. She gets to tell the sales staff how to make a presentation to clients and writes and edits material for the publications department.

On the other hand, at Persnickety Pastries, Inc., Jim is a 10-year veteran in the sales department, has lots of connections with clients who love him, but has sold almost zip in the last few years because he can't work the new computerized system. They make Jim Director of Client Communication to get him out of the way. Although he has the same vague title, he doesn't do as much as Jenny. Instead, he calls his old clients once in a while (who are now being serviced by reps who can sell) just to keep them happy. He might also sit in the booth at a trade show or take on other bench-warming duties.

When you find a vague title, ask around. There's usually a story behind it, and usually one that tells a lot about the company.

**Ultra Specific Titles** Here you've got the opposite situation, where Sheila's title is Director of Membership Recruitment and Josh is Director of Membership Literature. This might be evidence of a power struggle over who did what for the members. Keep in mind that you might be looking at the fossilized remains of this battle; it could have happened long before Sheila and Josh arrived. Finding out the facts, though, may tell you about the person who came up with the solution—a v.p., for example, who might still be there.

**Any Odd Title** If you spot somebody who's called "Special Assistant to the President" or "Director of Special Projects," you've probably found someone who has so much clout they were able to invent their own job and title. Or the president invented the job because she thought so highly of the person. Or it's the president's brother-in-law.

**The Hot Project Crew** Typically at a company you've heard about one project or product ad nauseam from your first day there. Practically the first words out of your boss's mouth during your interview before you were hired were about the Systemic Confabulation Processing Unit, or the SCPU for short. Look at the chart and see if you can figure out who's most involved in this project or product. If it's a group of departments, they can form a hierarchy that's independent of the chart. For example, you've got the crew who thunk up the SCPU, they're the hottest; then there's the marketing group that put together the plan that sold the thing; then there's the financial crowd that saved the day by getting the capital on short notice. The status of these departments may be out of proportion to their place on the chart, for at least as long as the SCPU is ripping along.

**The Dead Zone** The corollary to the above, of course, is the gang that bungled the last project or that does work that represents the company's past instead of its future. We're talking about the department in charge of manufacturing vinyl disks in a compact disk world.

**Other Oddities** You never know what kind of strange thing you might find on an organizational chart, but keep an eye out for weirdness. Don't accept that what's there has been created through a logical method. For example, see if there's a function that seems as if it should be performed by one department but that is split between two departments. I once worked at a place where the person who wrote the brochures and the person who designed them each worked for different bosses whose chain of command went up to separate vice presidents, all because of an ancient power struggle within the company. As a result, the publications were terrible until somebody suggested that one department should be formed to handle them. You might not be able to reorganize the company on your first day, but if you know where things could be improved you'll be ready to make that brilliant suggestion when the time comes.

## Power to the Person

Going over the organizational chart in detail will give you a good idea of who's got the power and who doesn't. But this will only give you an idea of who has sanctioned power—power that's been acknowledged by the system and incorporated into the formal structure. All this is hierarchical power, or power of position. Next you need to figure out who has personal power.

Keep in mind that many of those who are high on the chart have probably risen to their level of incompetence. They might have personal power—you'll remember that that's some ability, knowledge, or skill that people admire and that gets things done—or they may have started working beyond their capacity long ago. People who still have a good dose of personal power are the ones getting things done *now* and who are probably going to get promoted up the hierarchy sooner or later.

But not always. There are cases where someone has lots of ability, commands the respect of everyone around, gets things done, and yet has a boss who'd rather be run over by monster trucks than promote somebody who's acing the job. That doesn't mean, though, that you shouldn't learn what you can from the shooters and develop your own personal power.

But remember that personal power is just that—personal. It's something you've got that everybody else doesn't. It comes in thousands of flavors, and the trick is to realize what yours is instead of trying to mimic somebody else around you. It's easy to make the mistake of trying to emulate somebody else's personal power. You see it work for Sarah, and you figure this is a business skill that you can learn. So you mimic what Sarah does, and nothing happens.

A famous advertisement entitled "Brown's Job," written in 1920 for the BBDO advertising agency, illustrates this point rather nicely. I know it's old and crusty, but I like it, so here's some of it (pardon the sexism):

> Brown is gone, and many men in the trade are wondering who is going to get Brown's job.
>
> He never tried to sell anything. Brown wasn't exactly in the sales department. He visited with the distributors, called on a few dealers, once in a while made a little talk to a bunch of salesmen.

> Back at the office he answered most of the important complaints, although Brown's job wasn't to handle complaints. Brown's job wasn't in the credit department either, but vital questions of credit usually got to Brown, somehow or other. . . .
>
> Brown is gone, and men are now applying for Brown's job. Others are asking who is going to get Brown's job—bright, ambitious young men, dignified older men.
>
> Men who are not the son of Brown's mother, nor the husband of Brown's wife, nor the product of Brown's childhood—men who never suffered Brown's sorrows nor felt his joys, men who never loved the things that Brown loved nor feared the things he feared—are asking for Brown's job.
>
> Don't they know that Brown's chair and his desk, with the map under the glass top, and his pay envelope, are not Brown's job? Don't they know that they might as well apply to the Methodist Church for John Wesley's job?
>
> Brown's former employers know it. Brown's job is where Brown is.

Interestingly, the guy who wrote that ad—which became famous and recognized as one of the 100 greatest advertisements of all time—wasn't even a writer at BBDO. He was the treasurer.

So, look deep within thyself to see if you don't have a smidgen of the stuff. Here's what personal power looks like, so you can start figuring out who has it and what yours would look like if you apply it to your job:

**Likability** This quality tops the list because people who aren't likable have a hell of a time getting any other kind of personal power to work for them. Not that it's impossible—you'll always hear about the brilliant but terminally dorky guy that everyone turns to for techno advice but away from for anything else. But it's a major uphill battle.

In almost any organization there are some people running around whose only personal power is likability. They're not really good at anything, but they're such sweet, nice or interesting folks that people pay attention to them, take their weak ideas into consideration, and generally treat them with respect. Likability won't get you far all by itself, but without it you'll have a tough time getting anywhere.

It's not all that hard to be likable. Most people are likable most of the time. The point of telling you this is so you realize that you're not trying to be friendly at work just to be a smiley-faced facsimile of yourself but because *it's part of your job*. To put it bluntly, you have to work with other people, and to work well with them they have to like you, at least a little.

**Brains** Some people have power just because they're smart. Toss them into a situation they know nothing about and they see what others don't see. They can frame a problem logically, consider variables other people are blind to, and come up with a dozen possible solutions. People ask their opinion, and that gives them influence, which is power.

Realize, though, that these same people may be useless when it comes to making a good decision, acting quickly, or leading others—these are separate qualities. You might peg someone in your company as the thinker, but don't assume that means she's a mover and a shaker. She might just be supplying the movers and shakers with the solid ground upon which they move and shake.

As for you, if you've got it upstairs, use it to ease into the role of having Wisdom Beyond Your Years. The best way to do this is to tell people what you think, but not what to do. If your ideas are good, you'll be asked to join brainstorming meetings, and tossing out the winning idea at one of these thinkfests can be one of the fastest ways to get some pull.

**Talent** Like brains, this is something you're born with. You might see a guy in your office who can convince anybody he's got everything else on this list, even though he doesn't. The guy's a born actor, and his talent gives him power because people buy his line. You may spot people who are natural writers, designers, or entertainers. They draw others to them because their talent lets them deliver what others can't.

What've you got? Forget about what you think applies to your job—just think about your talent, and then find a way to use it at work. If you've got a good eye, use it to improve the look of your reports. People may start coming to you asking how they can make their reports look clearer, and that will open the door to other opportunities. Do you play a musical instrument? Hang on—I'm not going to tell you to truck your Steinway to the lobby to provide mood music for brass as they step out of the elevator. But if you let people know you're a musician, they may come to you for some advice when they're looking to hire someone to write the company's jingle or to hire entertainment for the company's annual party. This gets you working with a different group of people and helps demonstrate that there's more to you than the narrow definition of your job description. That's how coworkers begin to think of you as having the capability for larger roles.

**Skill** Some people at your work may have power because they have a wealth o' skills. Everybody flocks to Taja because she can make any software package on the planet do back flips. Or take Jake, who learned long ago how to work the purchasing department's system so that he gets his stuff before anybody else. These people have built personal power around their skills.

A skill, though, like cheese, is perishable—especially these days. A big mistake workin' folk make is to pin their hopes on their skill alone. Along comes software that anybody can use or a new manager in purchasing and whammo, your skill is, literally, history.

What you want to do is to get a skill that everybody will want to use you for but one that's not going to take a major hunk of your life to learn. Often these skills are like Jake's—some way of manipulating some part of the hierarchy or system. Zero in on one of these and become the expert. Be the only one who's figured out the bizarre filing system in the archives; the lone soul who can plan a good lunch celebration; or that special person who can use all the secret features of the voice mail system. Seemingly trivial skills like this will get you around people at all levels, and that's when you can move on to use some of your other personal powers.

Of course, you come through the door with a bag full of skills. Check your inventory to see if any skills you already have are exploitable. If you can fix a dead fax machine (in spite of what I told you in Chapter 4) let it be known that you're the Fax Master. One day the President will be standing over the cursed machine with a fist full of paper and a hang-dog face, and somebody will come and get you to rescue her. People have made v.p. for less.

**Knowledge** More and more, power in the Info Age is based on knowledge. But it's not the old-time "stock of knowledge" knowledge. And don't confuse it with talent or skill. A talent is an inborn ability; a skill is being able to repeat a task successfully. *Knowledge is information that can help turn a decision in the right direction.*

As time rolls on and knowledge increases and decisions have to be made faster and problems crop up quicker and ohmygodwe'vegottodosomething *fast* slams into everybody, your ability to get and turn over knowledge—no matter how low you sit in the hierarchy—will make or break your personal power quotient.

People where you work who have knowledge power probably have it based at least roughly on the structure of hierarchy. That is, Rich in Computers knows what's up with databases, and Leanna in Advertising knows the latest in demographic profiles. You have your own area, and it's obvious that you should keep up with what's going on as much as possible.

But one of the cool things about the knowledge revolution is that you don't have to just have knowledge about what you do. If you have useful knowledge about any aspect of the business, people will listen because everybody's desperate. If your boss is racking her brain saying "I just can't figure out where we can get slides made quickly for that presentation," and you say, "I just read about this new process where they can take a word processing file and output it in color onto slides," and it works, then you've saved the day.

What will ultimately give you knowledge power is if you make it a habit of having a grab bag of useful knowledge. You'll get known as someone who knows a lot about a variety of things.

**Vision** Some people can picture the future and go for it. The picture lets them visualize what needs to happen to create the future, and that serves both as a strong motivator and as a blueprint. Other people can't see the future until it's breathing down their neck.

Visionaries don't always have personal power though—and it has nothing to do with whether their view is accurate or not. A visionary has to present her vision in a way that appeals to people and gets them excited about achieving it.

When you run across a visionary in your organization, you have to evaluate the two things separately. First, do you think the vision is accurate? Can this realistically happen, and would it be everything it's cracked up to be? Second, can this visionary get the resources—people, time, and money—together to make it happen? If the person you're checking out falls short on either of these, then you're dealing with a minor visionary with a limited amount of personal power.

**Judgment** Good judgment is the ability to come up with a good decision by taking everything into consideration. People who can make good decisions look at the mix of brains, talent, skill, knowledge, and vision they have at their command and judge how valuable any piece of it is in relation to the other pieces and can figure out how far the mix will go toward solving the problem. It's a nifty trick, and much valued.

People with bad judgment, on the other hand, overrate or underrate part of the mix. Take, for example, a guy I'll call Lenny. He was in charge of the computer services in a company that was *built* on what computers could do. He had worked for the last ten years perfecting the operation of the big mainframe computer the company used for everything. He was smart, knowledgeable about what was going on in his field, and had lots of talent and skill. But he had no vision. When personal computers came along, he ignored them. Years went by, and he still insisted that everybody who worked there should have a terminal that hooked up to the main computer. In the meantime, other companies were using the latest and greatest software, which was only available on PCs.

Eventually the staff of one department brought in a load of Macintoshes—they had a good argument to, since they wanted to start desktop publishing—and Lenny tried to ignore that, too. Slowly it became obvious to everyone in the company that Lenny's judgment was bad. Questions began to be asked about how he was running the mainframe, which people had assumed (since they didn't know any better) was being well taken care of. And it wasn't long before hidden problems in the main computer setup were exposed.

At Occidental College, where I worked for several years, the head of the computer department, Tom Slobko, worked during the same years but had good judgment. He started with an IBM mainframe, moved to a Prime system that was much better, then took the college into the age of personal computers by not only making IBM PCs available but by providing training. Finally, when he saw that Macs were the way to go for some applications, he bought a load of them. What's more, he set up the system so all the computers could talk to each other. Unlike Lenny, Tom had good judgment, and a big part of it was vision.

But it wasn't vision alone that led Tom to the right decision. If he had just followed a vision of the future, he might have insisted on junking parts of the old system each time he moved on. Instead, he took into account all aspects of what worked and what didn't.

Although good judgment becomes more powerful with experience (especially experience specific to your company) some people will show it from the minute they walk in the door. These people will start having personal power as soon as they make their first good calls. You can improve your own judgment by hanging with them and seeing how their minds work. Sometimes you'll be amazed at what they take into consideration.

There's got to be something on this list that when you read it you said to yourself, "Yeah, I'm like that. The vision thing. That's me." Whatever it is, that's your wedge for power because that's what you're good at and—just as important—that's what you feel comfortable with. I'm not going to tell you to remake yourself into a skill-soaked bureaucracy manipulator if you aren't one, because it wouldn't work. Find what works, start with that, and add the others as you go. When you get promoted, don't forget that you want to stay in power not because of your position but because of your growing personal power.

Chapter 9

# What You've Got and What You're Supposed to Want

IN THIS CHAPTER WE'LL TALK ABOUT BENEFITS AND PERKS, RAISES AND PROMOTIONS, GETTING FIRED AND QUITTING, AND A FEW OTHER THINGS, BUT BEFORE THAT, LET'S GET RIGHT TO THE POINT AND TALK ABOUT THE SINGLE MOST IMPORTANT REASON YOU ARE WORKING AT ALL, AND THAT IS, OF COURSE, TO USE YOUR ENERGIES TO IMPROVE LIFE FOR THOSE IN OUR SOCIETY LESS FORTUNATE THAN—OH, WAIT A SEC. MAYBE IT'S NOT THAT. MAYBE IT'S MONEY.

## The Money

So how do you know if they're paying you enough? What are you worth? "You are worth *exactly the amount that would make you happy to take the job and not one penny less*. And you can take that to the bank," says Stanley Bing in *Crazy Bosses*. And I would add, when you are wondering what to ask for when it comes time for a raise, you are worth exactly the amount that will make you happy to keep working at your job, and not one penny less. If you don't think so, consider what you're giving the company. "As a worker," says Michael Ventura in the *L.A. Weekly,* "I am not an 'operating cost.' I am how the job gets done. I *am* the job. I am the company. Without me and my companion workers, there's nothing." Let's go over your contribution in detail. Here are a few things your employer gets from you:

**Your Time** Time ain't just money. Time is *life*. That's all we really have—a few hours here, a few hours there, and *pfft,* that's it. Just because the company might not think your time is all that valuable doesn't mean you should sell it cheap. I know there are practical considerations—they just don't pay junior associate assistant management trainees that much—but if you swallow the attitude that your time is cheap, you'll get screwed.

**Your Brains** The company is renting your head for the time you're at work, but it doesn't stop there. You may believe you can turn off jobthink when you walk out the door, but it ain't so. At the minimum, you'll be thinking about when you have to go back. You have to use your brain to plan your time to fit work in. You can't go out to the club tonight because you've got work tomorrow. So all those thoughts, feelings, and experiences you would've had at the club won't happen.

Beyond that, most people think about work problems when they're not at work. It's hard not to. If your brain cells weren't reworking yesterday's progress report they might be churning out the next megahit tune, or whatever it is that your brain cells can do.

**Your Emotions** Love it, hate it, either way your job is going to yank your heartstrings, buddy. You know the horror stories. You go home cranky and kick the cat, call your friends and whine, and they avoid you. Or you go home happy and excited, explaining to the cat how the Finster deal is almost closed because all your friends are sick of hearing you talk about work. Or you go home numb, and nothing seems fun.

And this leaves out all the wonder and trauma of what actually happens at work; all the relationships you have with the people there and how the company sculpts your emotional responses to help it make money, as I described in Chapter 7.

A company will, of course, never mention that they're buying all this—that would weaken their bargaining position. Besides, companies don't like to get touchy-feely. It's not quantifiable. You can't run a cost analysis on it. So it goes unsaid. But you shouldn't let it go without giving it a good deal of thought. Bing says, "Beyond a certain minimum sum, you're looking for an amount that allows you to feel that you have just received good value for the sale of you."

## The Benies

Before you fly into a rage after reading the last section and decide that you sold out cheap, take a look at the other stuff you're getting in what's known as your "compensation package."

**Medical Coverage** If you've got decent health coverage, that's costing your employer major bucks. Then you should include it into the price you're selling yourself for.

There are basically three approaches to health coverage: the health maintenance organization (better known as an HMO), the preferred provider organization (PPO), and traditional indemnity insurance. In an HMO, you see their doctors. You flash your membership card to get in and usually have to pay very little or nothing for your care. Your choice is only among their doctors, but you get comprehensive care for minimum cost.

In the preferred provider deal, you can go to any doctor you want, but if you choose from the ones on the company's list (these are the "preferred providers") then it costs you less. Either way, you pay the doctor the full amount and then you're reimbursed by the company. In this plan you get more choice than in an HMO, but the plans are typically more expensive.

Traditional indemnity insurance lets you select any doctor—there's no preferred list. You pay and are reimbursed by the company. This setup gives you maximum choice for maximum cost.

You may work for a company that gives you a choice of medical plans; if so, look carefully at the fine print—certain plans will exclude certain kinds of care. HMOs are by far the best deal for new careersters because you get the most complete coverage for the cheapest rate. You'd only want one of the others if you have an unusual condition that requires you to go to a particular specialist.

**Vacation Days** Normally you'll get a minimum number of vacation days your first year and then more after you've been there a few years. A typical range would be to get one week your first year and to eventually get four weeks after, say, five years.

Some companies require that you work there three to six months or longer before you can take your vacation time. Others let it accumulate per pay period, so you can take however much you have.

**Sick Days** You'll get a certain number of days a year to be sick—five is typical. Some companies make all of them available at the beginning of the year; in others, they accumulate with each pay period, so for every 80 hours you work you get, say, 0.2 days of sick time. Many companies convert them to vacation days after they accumulate above a certain minimum.

**Religious Holidays** Religious holidays that aren't part of our Great American Heritage are often handled by giving employees personal days that they can use as they please—for Yom Kipper or whatever. You might get five of these a year. These usually don't accumulate; unused days drop off at the end of the year.

**Comp Time** This is time off given to you in exchange for extra hours that you put in—as compensation; thus, "comp time." Some companies keep track of this through a formal system; in others, the boss just gives you a few hours off if you worked over the weekend.

**Parental Leave** Business is finally recognizing the importance of one human activity that might be considered important: procreation. The general direction companies are going is to let you off for three months without pay to have a kid (whether you're going to be a mom or a dad). You can cover part of this with whatever sick time or vacation time you have.

**Other Kinds of Time Off** Some places are nuts about defining every possible kind of time off. The worst case of this I ever saw was when I was working for a city government. In addition to sick time and vacation time, there was family medical time (for when kids got sick), individual time (for religious holidays of your choice), and dental time. The city insisted on keeping track of all these times separately—I know, because that was my job as payroll clerk. Of course, it didn't exactly work out that way. Typically I'd get a phone call and the conversation would go like this:

> Joe: Hey, Garrett, put me down for two weeks vacation starting August 14th. Me and the wife are taking the kids to Disney World.
>
> Me: That sounds cool, Joe. Let me check this out . . . hmm, looks like you've only got seven days vacation.
>
> Joe: Really? What else do I have?
>
> Me: Let's see . . . looks like two days family medical, two days individual, and three days sick.
>
> Joe: What about dental?
>
> Me: Your long weekend in Aspen.
>
> Joe: Oh, yeah, right, right, I forgot. O.K., let's see. Why don't you give me five days vacation, two days family medical, one day individual, and two days sick.
>
> Me: You got it. Have a good time.

A lot of companies now realize that it doesn't matter what you take time off for, so the move is toward fewer defined days.

Occasionally you'll also find a place that offers some unusual time off. I once worked for a hospital that wished to be perceived as "having a heart," and so we all got Valentine's Day and our birthdays off—a nice touch, especially the birthday.

Some places will be very casual about the time off you take. It'll be up to your boss to keep track of it, although more often it's now kept track of on computer and printed out each pay period.

## The Perks

Companies have a number of "fringe benefits," sometimes of only minor interest, other times good enough to make you pick one job over another. It's also not beyond imagination that you may suggest some of these if your company doesn't offer them. After all, it makes the company more attractive to good employees, and sometimes it costs the company little or nothing to offer them. Here are some you might run into:

**A Legal Tax Dodge** If you pay a bunch of tax-deductible costs out of your paycheck, such as medical care or child care, there's a nifty little trick many companies are starting to use: they take these costs out of your paycheck before they withhold your taxes. This makes your income smaller, which makes your withholding smaller. If the money they take out goes to cover a company medical plan, they apply it, and you don't have to worry about it. If it goes to child care, you have to estimate at the beginning of the year what you're going to spend on child care; they then put that money in a separate account, and you get reimbursed out of that account for any child care costs you spend during the year. If everything works out, you spend exactly the amount you estimated.

These programs are usually administered by separate financial management companies that do all the paperwork; your company doesn't have to mess with it and they don't even have to pay any money for it. The financial management service makes its money by generating interest on the funds they hold throughout the year.

**Direct Deposit Pay** Going to the bank to deposit your paycheck is a pain, and a lot of employers have eliminated this problem by offering to deposit your paycheck directly into your bank. Usually this results in your money getting there faster—not only do you not have to walk your paycheck over to the bank, many payroll departments process their direct deposits first, so the money can get there the day before pay day.

**Getting to Work: Parking Lots, Buses, Trains, Carpools** In some parts of the country, especially where public transportation sucks and everybody drives, parking is a major deal. You might have to pay for your own transportation, or, in more progressive companies, they'll pay. In really progressive companies, you'll get a transportation allowance. If you want to apply it to parking, fine; or you can carpool with a friend, split the parking costs and pocket the rest; or you can ride a bike and keep the whole amount. In southern California and other places where traffic is a real problem, companies will offer even more incentives to keep you from driving alone to work. (Some metropolitan areas have laws that require employers to encourage alternatives to solo commuting.) These might be subsidized vanpools, prime parking places for carpoolers, or reduced rates for public transportation. If your company doesn't offer any of these and you think they should, you can get information by writing to Commuter Transportation Services, Inc., a company that has pioneered these alternatives in the Los Angeles area. Their address is 3550 Wilshire Boulevard, Suite 300, Los Angeles, CA 90010.

**Flexible Weeks** A working alternative that's becoming more common is working a traditional 40-hour week in less time. In one version, you work four ten-hour days. In another, you work what's known as a nine-eighty; that is, you work eighty hours in nine days, so you have a three-day weekend every other week.

Either of these arrangements makes for a long haul, but most people that try them love them. For one thing, in some cases this actually *reduces* your overall hours. It's easy for a normal eight-hour day to stretch to ten, and you may wind up working them a few days every week. If you change your schedule so you officially work a ten-hour day and officially have the last day off, your overall time stays pretty close to forty hours.

Another alternative that falls under the category of flexible hours is coming in and leaving at nonstandard times. This was also pioneered in California to help reduce the squash of the traditional rush hours on the freeway. With this setup you might come in at ten and leave at seven.

Just because your company doesn't officially offer these arrangements doesn't mean you can't suggest them. If you think you have a hard sell, you may want to get some literature on these workstyles (also available from Commuter Transportation Services, whose address is listed a few paragraphs above).

**Telecommuting or Working at Home** This is the latest boon to workers brought on by the technological revolution. Your company may even have a telecommuting program in place.

Strictly speaking, you don't need to have a computer to work at home. If you need to review some reports and have a day's worth of work, you might ask the boss if you can do it at home, away from distractions. To make a regular habit of it, though, most people will need a computer they can work on that is capable of transferring their work to the computer at work. Having a modem and a fax machine also help connect you electronically to your employer.

If you've got a benevolent boss, it may be easy to suggest telecommuting, and I advise doing this not long after you first get your job (see Chapter 4, *In Your Face: The First Few Weeks).*

**Learning** Business wants you to keep learning and will sometimes pay for it. If you see your fellow workers running off to workshops or weeklong training seminars, find out what the deal is—the sooner the better. (See my advice in Chapter 4, *In Your Face: The First Few Weeks.)*

If you've got a hankering to go back to school, ask if your employer will give you an extended leave of absence—many will. If your schooling will apply to your job, it's a good deal for the company because they get a new, improved employee without having to search for one. Some will even foot part of the bill.

If your company doesn't offer any kind of educational opportunities at all, then you've got to resort to self-training, which I describe in the Little Extras section below.

**Travel** Going places for work can be a perk or a drag, depending on what you like. The problem is that you may be flying to beautiful downtown San Francisco, but all you see of it is the inside of a hotel. Sure, you can sometimes attach some vacation days to a business trip, but that's the exception, not the rule. To really like business travel, you have to like dragging luggage through airports, riding in cabs, and staying in strange hotel rooms. I have to admit that sometimes I'm in the mood—but I wouldn't want to make a career out of it. You may be different.

## The Little Extras

Aside from the official list of benefits and perks, there are, in every office, unofficial benefits of the job. They're not talked about because some, if pushed too far, are disruptive, unethical, illegal, or all three. All of them involve the question of degree. If you are of unbending moral principle, then they'll seem shady and you won't want to do any of them. For the rest of us, though, it's a question of how much we indulge.

**Personal Phone Calls** Undoubtedly the most innocuous of the secret benefits is the ability to get a brief personal call or to make one. If your company is tight about this, you're in a strict company. About the only thing worse is if they frisk you for pencils on the way out the door.

In most places, you don't have to worry about making a necessary call, like to find out when the mechanic is going to be done with your car or to make a doctor's appointment. Even calling a friend is usually O.K.—you probably only want to do this if you're making plans and it's the only time you can easily talk, although some places will tolerate a ten-minute call where you're obviously just chatting. It just depends on the culture. In nearly all cultures, though, spouses are exempt from the usual rules—they have special privileges; its often even seen as a good thing if you talk to your spouse—stable young person with a sense of family, and all that.

Long-distance calls are, of course, a different matter. In some companies, making a toll call is grounds for being taken out behind the Coke machine and being caned to within an inch of your life. At other places, they literally don't care, because the company makes so many long distance calls that they simply pay a huge flat rate to make all the calls they want.

**Supplies** My late father-in-law of blessed memory was possibly the most honest man I have ever known. He could not prevent the company's pens and pencils from coming home with him; they would seem to just appear in the top pocket of his business shirt. But when he found one, he would put it in a separate drawer he had for the purpose, wrapping it with the others, all held in a bundle with a rubber band. When he remembered, he'd take the most recent bundle back to work, and then begin a new one in a few days when another pen would appear.

For most of us, this is far beyond the call of duty. Pens, pencils, memo pads and the like are just the flotsam and jetsam that flow back and forth between work and home. Unless it's hugely abused—people taking reams of copy paper home to feed their laser printer—neither companies nor employees worry much about it, and you shouldn't either.

**Office Services** If you need to use the copy machine to make one copy of something for yourself, nobody is going to say anything. The same is probably true for faxing something, printing out your personal computer file on your laser printer at work, or having the mail room send out a personal package for you. Again, it's a matter of degree—how often do you use these resources and how much time and money do you chew up each time? There's no standard answer—it differs with each company—but you can be pretty sure that a little won't hurt and that virtually everybody else is doing it some, and besides, is it really too much to ask considering you ran that errand for the company and didn't bother to turn in your mileage? Just try to keep your accounts even and your conscience clear.

**Self-Training** In companies that can't afford to—or won't—send you for training on something (usually these days, it's software) then I think you're justified in some secret self-training. It works like this: you've got a software package you're using and you kinda know how to run it. You also know you're doing a lot of things the hard way. Since the hard way is the way you know, it's the dependable way. It may be slow, but not as slow as if you took hours to learn the faster way. Self-training is when you decide to learn the faster way, knowing that in the short term you'll be performing your task much more slowly, but also knowing that you'll be able to do it faster next time.

You may have to actually hide the fact that you're doing this from your boss, who wants the job *now*. But in the long run you're helping the company: You're becoming a more valuable, capable employee, and you'll save time eventually. More importantly, you're helping yourself. In the employee-employer bargain, one of the most important things you're receiving in exchange for your work is experience. It's something the company owes you—think of it as part of your pay. If you don't take it, you're cheating yourself.

This doesn't just apply to software. In any skill you want to learn, there's a learning curve, and a good company will be willing to support you as you go through it. One of the arguments you might run across from a less than enlightened employer is that "it's not part of your job." Weigh this carefully. Is it not part of your job because it's a function that doesn't apply to what you do, or is it not part of your job because your boss or someone else wants to keep the more advanced skills from you? Answer that, and do what you need to do.

**Kids at Work** It's more common these days to see tikes roaming the halls of an office, and a good thing, too, if you ask me. There's nothing that humanizes a power desk more quickly than a kid slobbering on it. The practice has been at least officially recognized with the growing popularity of Bring Your Daughter to Work Day. Since many employers refuse to address child care as a basic human need, both moms and dads have found times when they simply had no choice but to show up with their kids. Some employers won't tolerate this at all, but with others, it's a question of how much the kids distract you and others from work. That's a function of what kind of place you work at, how old your kids are, how often you bring them, and what their typical behavior is.

There is probably no official policy on bringing kids to work, and if there is, it's likely to be negative. Ask someone you trust what the deal is. Or, if you're brave, strike a blow for humanness: bring little Jordan in, and act like everything's normal. Introduce your kid to everyone, starting with your boss. If anybody gives you trouble, tell them you didn't know it was against the rules.

**Loose Hours** Some places will just generally not try to monitor your coming and going and will regard this as an unspoken perk. The attitude is usually expressed in the boss-uttered phrase, "I don't care when you're here as long as you get your work done." There are bosses who will say this and not mean a word of it (they *want* to be nice, but they just can't) but most who do say it mean it—within reason. It's an expression of trust. They want to see dedication, but they won't be upset if you take an occasional long lunch, run to the cleaners in the middle of the afternoon, or come in an hour late after a long day before. What they don't like is feeling like you're exploiting their generosity.

If your boss seems liberal-minded with your hours, go ahead and use the time *but at first always tell her where you'll be and how long you'll be gone*. This is simply returning the trust placed in you. You're sending the message that you're using the time for legitimate personal reasons, not just that you're ditching. If you disappear for three hours with no explanation, even the most tolerant boss will get steamed, probably because his boss will ask where you are.

After some time, it may not be necessary to tell your boss about every fifteen-minute absence, but it's still a good idea with the longer leaves.

**Hooky** Those of you who are among the chronically obligated may not want to read this part, for I am about to suggest that it is actually O.K. if you call in sick sometimes *when you don't even feel bad*. Yes, that's right—ditch work.

This can be an amazingly revitalizing act. You look outside and the weather's beautiful. There's not much going on at work—in fact, it's kinda slow. Suddenly, you are seized with the feeling that you need to allow yourself to simply *go out and be in the world.* And you know what? That is a perfectly healthy, sane, and enriching thing to do. My personal opinion is that anyone who has never done this has some serious mental problems.

If you decide to go for it, do it right. Try to be considerate of the people back at work. First, don't run off on a day that you know will be extra tough for everyone back at the ranch without you there. That's just a crappy way to treat your coworkers. Second, don't try to get someone to lie for you. Don't call even your best friends at work and tell them that you're ditching. Even if they don't have to explain your absence, they're in the awkward position of knowing if anybody asks. And third, when you call in, don't go on with an elaborate and suspicious-sounding story about your pituitary gland or some other weird ailment. Just say you're feeling under the weather. If it's really a slow day, no one is going to question you. You're entitled to your sick days. No one wants to be suspicious of you, and they won't be unless you cook up some giant fable.

If you have that rare kind of pathological boss that delights in exposing your innocent charade, you have to take a more devious approach—or deprive yourself of your day of rest, which I don't recommend, since with a boss like that you probably need it. So here's what you do: get sick at work the day before you want to take off. This is especially good if you want to take off Friday, which is suspicious in itself. Go into work on Thursday as usual, but start complaining first thing. When somebody says "Good morning, how are you," just say, "I'm fine. I think I might be coming down with something, though." Then sniffle. Get progressively worse, looking sort of dazed as you walk through the hallways, saying "What? I'm sorry, I'm having trouble concentrating," when people talk to you. Finally, about two o'clock, go to your boss and say, "I'm sorry, but I've got to go home. I feel horrible." Voilá. You're set up for your day off and you got out early. I have never actually pulled this stunt, of course, but I hear it works.

## What You're Supposed to Want

All of the above is what you've got—but you're not supposed to be happy with it. That is, you're not supposed to be content. Business wants you to be ambitious, because that way you'll work hard to get more of what it has to offer. So what more does it have to offer? What is it that it wants you to want?

This is very simple. What you're supposed to want is more money, a bigger office, and more power over more people. If that sounds good to you, then you're properly motivated as far as the business world is concerned. If this doesn't sound that exciting, and you had in mind things like personal accomplishment or a feeling of satisfaction or making the world a better place to live in, then you'll have to watch out for yourself. You can get these things, but it's up to you. They won't come automatically with success, as the other stuff will.

This is so because, as I've mentioned a few times, business doesn't really understand much about what makes humans tick. It just goes along making money, fitting people in where it can. To get what you want you've got to make a bargain with business in terms it understands. Those things are money, time (which is money), and your exploitable talents and skills (which is also money).

But before you can strike any bargains, business has to be convinced that you've increased in value since they hired you, something most employers do at regularly scheduled interviews.

**How They Figure Out How Much More to Give You** *You* will not be evaluated. Your *performance* will be evaluated.

This evaluation will be called your review. Sort of the way Bono's performance is reviewed.

There are dozens of systems to evaluate people, including the "I like you, Francis, how about a big fat raise?" system. Most companies have dispensed with that one, though, and many give managers a framework within which to evaluate performance. It's like a report card, except that instead of subjects there are categories like, "productivity," "innovation," "resourcefulness," and "cooperation." There's a scale on which you're graded in each category: one to ten, or whatever. There is usually a written part of the evaluation, too, where your boss says glowing things about you.

The words may sound nice, but it's the numbers that matter, because companies that use systems like this are trying to standardize the evaluation so that Ben, the smooth talking layabout in shipping, doesn't talk his way into a fifty percent raise while Doris, the shy but efficient marketing whiz, has to make do with a five percent hike. Often companies regulate raises by using a merit pool. That's where all the money the company has for raises is viewed as a giant tank o' dough that's doled out according to who's most deserving. So, depending on the money available, everybody with a score of eight and above gets a fifteen percent raise; everybody from six to eight gets a twelve percent raise, and so forth, until the money's all used up.

The merit pool, though, depends on the idea that there will be a fairly predictable distribution of scores. If everybody in the company gets a score of nine, then everybody is supposed to get a fifteen percent raise, which adds up to more money than is in the pool.

The people who plan these things try very hard to keep this from happening in the first place. But when a personnel manager begins to see too many high reviews coming in, she's liable to have a little talk with certain managers. "Do you think he *really* deserves this nine?" she says to your boss, and before you know it, you're tossed out of the deep end of the pool quicker than a four-year-old without a life jacket. Sad but true.

This all happens before you get a look at your review, of course, but it brings up an important point. When you get your review, you may have the feeling it's cast in stone. That isn't true. You're asked to sign the review if you accept it, but you definitely shouldn't if you don't think it's fair. Most companies have a procedure for employees who protest their scores, and it's not unusual for the scores to be adjusted. If you argue that your score is too low, for all you know you're helping your boss go back to the personnel manager and say, "See? He knows he deserves a nine, just as I scored him before you talked me out of it."

**Could I Have Some More Time, Sir?** So, let's say you've been doing well at your job and your reviews look good. You figure that you'll be offered a raise and maybe even a promotion pretty soon. This is the time you start thinking about how you can bargain with the company, because by offering you a raise or promotion they are telling you that you are more valuable to the company and they're willing to compensate you for it. What you want to do is to have some control over that compensation.

Because work takes so much time out of your life, that might be one of the first things you ask for. It's becoming more popular for employees to ask to take more time off in lieu of a raise, so you can try this first if it appeals to you. Don't be surprised if your boss balks, though. Even though it sounds perfectly logical, time doesn't equate directly to money from an employer's point of view. Because they already have a big investment in you—primarily training and benefits—it's most economical for a company to have you work as much as possible. But you may be in a situation where the company needs the cash it would save by not giving you a raise more than it needs you during the two extra weeks of vacation you're suggesting. So try it. They won't do anything except say no.

If they do say no, try negotiating a sabbatical—that is, time off without pay. It will always sound better if you tell them why you need a sabbatical—to compose the third movement of your symphony, for example, or to research your family tree—but you don't have to. You should try for this in *addition* to getting a raise, not instead of a raise. As the company sees it, you'll cost more per hour but that will be somewhat offset by the month or so sabbatical when they don't have to pay you. Again, expect them to say no.

If you're interested in more personal time, you should at least bring up the subject the first time you're offered a raise or promotion so you've set a precedent. If they won't say yes this time, maybe they will next time.

**Can I Do That—It Looks Funner?** If it's personal satisfaction you're after, you need to plot out a long-range plan, one that might even take you out of the company. When you know where you want to go, you'll be able to tell if what they're offering is on your map or not.

Let's say you're interested in product development but you were hired in the direct mail advertising department. If you're offered a promotion, ask instead if you can get transferred over to the department where you want to be. If not, then ask if some of your new duties can include working more closely with product development so you can do a better job with the direct mail pieces. If not, as a last resort, see if your title can be changed to something that will look better on your resume for the direction you're trying to go.

**So, Alina, how would you like to be *senior* assistant associate management trainee?** A promotion can be a wonderful thing. If you're moved up into a spot that gives you more money and more control over your activities and allows you to do more of what you want to, you don't need me to tell you that's a good thing. My job is to bring out the less obvious—things to think about before you grab that fancy new title.

The first question to ask yourself is, is my strong young body just one more to be shoved in front of some freight train of a problem that can't be stopped? If nobody stays long in the position, that might be the case.

Next question: does this change move you toward your career goal or away from it? Flattering as it may be to step up to assistant copywriter, if you really want to be a journalist, moving up in advertising ain't gonna get you there.

Finally, if you're offered any kind of management position, you have to face the age-old question: do you want to do, or do you want to supervise the doing? A lot of people become bosses only to find they hate bossing people and wish they were back in the trenches doing the real work.

## What You Definitely Don't Want

Sometimes bad things happen to good people. That's what this section's about—losing jobs.

## I'm A Loser Baby, So Why Don't Ya Fire Me

There aren't many companies left where Mr. Spacely storms into the office and shouts, "Jetson, your FIRED!" Normally this can only happen if you get caught committing a major employment crime, like stealing from the company or taking drugs at work.

These days there are a lot of laws about why you can and can't fire somebody. For one thing, women, minorities, and men over forty are in what is referred to by personnel staff as a "protected class," which means that people in these groups tend to be discriminated against in employment practices. This means that if an employer wants to fire someone belonging to one of these groups, the employer has to show that it was not because of discrimination. So companies usually follow a pretty strict procedure so they can protect their assets. This is called "building a case," and the goal is to document your poor performance (and nothing but) with a nice, thick stack of paper. The usual drill is this:

**Warnings** Warnings start out verbally. Your boss will tell you that you didn't do such a swell job on the Higgens report. Eventually, these chats will become more serious, reaching The Official Warning, which is, in so many words, you must improve your performance to keep working here.

At some point, a warning will be committed to writing. The usual place for this is on a performance review, which you sign—thus acknowledging that you realize you must improve or you'll get the ax. Sometimes, though, a boss will want to move faster and won't want to wait for a scheduled performance review. If that's the case then you'll get a letter that you will also be asked to sign.

Keep in mind that your boss will probably start writing down notes about your chats together before you actually get a written warning. That way the company has a longer record of your becoming a problem. You should keep notes too so you don't get ambushed. Too many bosses think they've delivered a clear verbal warning and write up their notes that way, when in fact they beat around the bush so much you have no idea that they're trying to tell you to do better. Without your own notes, taken at the time, you've got nothing to contradict their version.

If your performance fails to improve, your boss can take one of two steps. She can, if she feels she's built a good enough case, fire you. Or, she can put you on probation.

**Probation** The idea behind probation is supposedly to give you a time period in which to shape up or you'll be shipped out. Sometimes this is the genuine purpose, and if you do shape up, you can stay—often it's just another step in building a case against you. Your boss knows he wants you gone, and the probation is just another, bigger nail in your coffin.

In a typical probation period, you're given a written list of performance problems you're supposed to fix. A schedule is also set up: every week or two your boss and you will sit down to talk over your performance. If your boss is just trying to get rid of you, these can be hell, because no matter how much better you do your boss will find fault with it, and that's what will go on the report. If your boss is truly interested in your improvement, and you do improve, then everybody can feel better about it.

Sometimes getting put on probation is a mercy gesture. Your boss may feel she has a good case to fire you already, but instead of that, she puts you on probation, with an unspoken message that says, "you're going to get blown out of here, so you might want to quit before we get you." If this is what you can read between the lines, then brush up your resume and use your probation period to look for another job.

Because the firing process usually takes a while, you might decide you'll be better off if you resign. Often a boss will be so grateful that you've spared him the pain of firing you that he'll even give you a good recommendation for your next job. It's no skin off his nose, as long as he just talks about your strengths and not your weaknesses.

You should be aware, though, that to collect unemployment, you have to have been fired or laid off. If you quit, you can't collect.

**Life After the Firing Squad** If you get fired, you might think that your next employer will call your old boss and get an earful of all the ways you botched your job. This usually isn't the case because there are laws that protect you against this type of negative talk. Companies are afraid if they talk you down you'll come back with a law suit against them. The way personnel departments handle it is this: when they get a call from somebody checking out your resume, they only give three pieces of information: they confirm the dates that you worked there, they'll confirm what you got paid if asked (they won't volunteer it) and, if asked, they'll say whether they would hire you again—the answer to which, if you were fired, is no. So your potential employer will know you were fired, but won't know why. That's why it's important to admit in an interview that you have been fired—and offer a good reason why. Here are a few:

- MY BOSS WAS INCOMPETENT • You don't come right out and say this. You broadly hint that this is so. Something like, "Although I worked well with the staff and even with the vice president, I felt my immediate supervisor wasn't handling the department very well. I did what I could, but eventually he asked me to leave."

- THE COMPANY WAS BACKWARDS • Again, imply; don't be specific. "I was trying to develop some new procedures, but these went against the grain there. They had an approach they'd used for years, and even though they knew it needed to be improved, they disagreed with my ideas." If you use this, you should back it up.

- THE POSITION DIDN'T FIT ME • "The duties of the position that were described to me were not the ones they asked me to carry out. The job didn't use my strengths."

**Things Not to Say** Don't admit your incompetence. Don't say, "I guess it's true that I couldn't get those reports in on time. But I know I'd be a lot better this time around."

**Getting Laid Off** There's no shame in getting laid off, even though it feels like it. Here's something to watch for, though: if your company looks like it's in trouble, get your resume out there and don't trust anything your company tells you. They may announce that layoffs won't begin until July, that only ten percent of the staff will go, that everyone will get a fat severance package, and then something goes wrong.

Remember Harsh Reality Number One: companies must make money. The corollary for this is they have to avoid losing money. That means if the hammer comes down on them, they might not have the ability to deliver on their promises. One company I know of saw it was going to lose funding and based on that told the employees what to expect several months down the road. But the road caved in, and a whole slew of people were booted out with nothing. Their recourse was to lump it.

## That's It! I'm Outta Here!

Ready to quit? So soon? O.K., maybe you've been at your job for a while. Traditional wisdom is that you shouldn't quit a job too soon because it looks bad on your resume. That depends. If you move up to a much better job, it just shows that you're ambitious and can take advantage of situations that come along. Even if you take another job that's not a big move up, employers will generally be O.K. with it as long as you have a decent reason. It's when you start accumulating a record of six-month job hops that it begins to look bad.

If you're quitting, I'll bet it's for one of the reasons below.

**You Get a Better Job** An enlightened boss will be happy for you if you get a better job somewhere else, and even the worst boss will suddenly become enlightened when you tell them this. The reason is that she knows you suddenly hold all the cards. What good would it do for her to yell at you? You're just going to leave anyway. So your boss will probably support you.

The times a boss won't is when he has a legitimate reason to be pissed: you're giving too short notice or you quit too soon after being hired. Sometimes you can't help this. If a really good opportunity comes along and the position needs to be filled as soon as possible, then you've got to take it—but avoid it if you can. See if you can't make your new employer wait. After all, if they see you betray your old employer, they know you'd do the same to them.

**You're Going Back to School** Like getting a better job, most bosses will be behind you if you've decided to return to the comfy halls of academia. As I mentioned earlier in this chapter, see if your employer will grant you an extended leave of absence so you can get your old job back when you're out.

**You Just Can't Stand Your Job Anymore** Sometimes you feel you've got to quit just because the job is destroying your mind. You know if you do you'll face poverty and the prospect of looking for a job without having a job, which doesn't look good. Still, some jobs can be so emotionally damaging that no amount of money is worth it. It doesn't matter how bad they say the job market is—what's the use of having a job if it means your entire existence is a living hell? What? You're not sure if your job is a living hell or not? The next chapter will help you decide.

Chapter 10

# Satisfaction: The Work and Life Thing

THERE'S BEEN A LOT OF TALK, ESPECIALLY AMONG BABY BOOMERS, ABOUT HOW YOU BALANCE WORK AND LIFE. RIGHT NOW YOU MIGHT BE MORE WORRIED ABOUT HOW TO JUST FUNCTION AT WORK, BUT YOU'D BETTER PAY ATTENTION OR YOU, LIKE MILLIONS OF BOOMERS, WILL FIND YOURSELF SUCKED INTO A WORKING LIFE YOU HATE.

First off, let's take a long look. Human beings have filled their lives with work in different proportions since we crawled out of the muck, and one of the easiest mistakes to make is to think that the amount of work we do and how it fits into life has been perfected to some kind of peak by scientific progress. The propaganda is that in all past eons humans have worked harder and longer, starved anyway half the time, and on top of that were miserable because they didn't have the nice things we have like plumbing and Nintendo. It ain't so. Harvard economist Juliet Schor points this out in her book *The Overworked American* (Basic Books):

> The lives of so-called primitive peoples are commonly thought to be harsh—their existence dominated by the "incessant quest for food." In fact, primitives do little work. By contemporary standards, we'd have to judge them extremely lazy. If the Kapauku of Papua work one day, they do no labor on the next. !Kung Bushmen put in only two and a half days per week and six hours per day. In the Sandwich Islands of Hawaii, men work only four hours per day. And Australian aborigines have similar schedules.

But what about once civilization got a foothold? Didn't the Greeks break their backs building all those temples? Nope:

> Leisure time in Ancient Greece and Rome was also plentiful. Athenians had fifty to sixty holidays annually, while in Tarentum they apparently had half the year. In the old Roman calendar, 109 of 355 days were designated *nefasti,* or "unlawful for judicial and political business." By the mid-fourth century, the number of *feriae publicae* (public festival days) reached 175.

Well then surely by the Middle Ages the peasants were sweating like dogs through a horrendous work day. Uh-uh. Schor again:

> A thirteenth-century estimate finds that whole peasant families did not put in more than 150 days per year on their land. Manorial records from fourteenth-century England indicate an extremely short working year—175 days—for servile laborers. Later evidence for farmer-miners, a group with

control over their work time, indicates they worked only 180 days a year.

So what happened? The Industrial Revolution, that's what. And by the 1800s, everything you've heard about sixteen-hour days in rotten conditions was true. Employers not only thought they had bought most of a worker's time, they thought they had bought the worker and had the right to dictate all kinds of insane behavior. Take, for example, this list of employee rules for people who worked at the *Boston Herald* in 1872 (taken from *The Book of Business Anecdotes* by Peter Hay, Wing Books):

1. Office employees each day will fill lamps, clean chimneys, and trim wicks. Wash windows once a week.
2. Each clerk will bring in a bucket of water and a scuttle of coal for the day's business.
3. Make your pens carefully. You may whittle nibs to your individual taste.
4. Men employees will be given an evening off each week for courting purposes, or two evenings a week if they go regularly to church.
5. After thirteen hours of labor in the office, the employee should spend the remaining time reading the Bible and other good books.
6. Every employee should lay aside from each pay day a goodly sum of his earnings for his benefit during his declining years so that he will not become a burden to society.
7. Any employee who smokes Spanish cigars, uses liquor in any form, or frequents pool and public halls or gets shaved in a barber shop, will give good reason to suspect his worth, intentions, integrity, and honesty.
8. The employee who has performed his labor faithfully and without fault for five years, will be given an increase of five cents per day in his pay, providing profits from business permit it.

The only thing that brought hours under control, says Schor, is that people, in the form of labor unions, said *we're not going to take this anymore*. Hours eventually were reduced to a reasonable level.

But by then the model of work—which is based on the idea of a factory where you're paid for your time instead of for what you do—had taken a firm hold and is with us today. It's been a battle between capitalism, which needs to make workers efficient, and people, who need space for inefficient, unproductive time like hanging out with friends or being with family members.

The labor union's efforts kept hours down until the 1940s, when they picked up again. And the pace got faster and faster. Schor says that Americans have added about nine hours a year to the amount they work since the 1970s because of corporate pressure:

> The golden age of the 1950s and 1960s was followed by oil price increases, a slowdown in productivity growth, heightened international competition, and sluggish demand. Corporate profits, which had been at record highs, fell substantially. Recessions became deeper and more damaging. Businesses were under increasing pressure to cut costs and improve profit margins. Predictably, a large portion of the burden was "down-loaded" onto employees—particularly during the 1980s, when the squeeze on many U.S. corporations hit hardest. Their strategy has been to require workers to do more for less.

The point of all this history is to convince you of one fact: If you grew up in the 1970s and 1980s, then you weren't seeing anything like normal human work behavior—not for any preceding time in human history or even for other times in America. What you saw was flat-out, full-tilt, working madness. If you've never liked the idea of working like the yupped-out Boomers of the eighties but felt that this is just business as usual in America, think again. Lots of Boomers are now realizing just how bad things have gotten, and they're complaining. Loudly. Michael Ventura, writing the *L.A. Weekly*, just snapped:

> It was during the years of office work that I caught on: I got two weeks' paid vacation per year. A year has 52 weeks. Even a comparatively unskilled, uneducated worker like me, who couldn't (still can't) do fractions or long division—even I had enough math to figure that two goes into 52 . . . how many times? Twenty-six. Meaning it would take me 26 years on the job to accumulate one year for myself. And I could only have that year in 26 pieces, so it wouldn't even feel like a year. In other words, no time was truly mine. My boss merely allowed me an illusion of freedom, a little space in which to catch my breath, in between the 50 weeks that I lived but *he* owned. My employer uses 26 years of my life for every year I get to keep. And what do I get in return for this enormous thing I am giving? What do I get in return for my *life?* A paycheck that's as skimpy as they can get away with. If I'm lucky, some heath insurance. (If I'm *really* lucky, the employer's definition of "health" will include my teeth and my eyes—maybe even my mind.) And, in a truly enlightened workplace, just enough pension or "profit-sharing" to keep me sweet but not enough to make life different. And that's it.
>
> . . . It seems an odd way to structure a free society: Most people have little or no authority over what they do five days a week for 45 years. Doesn't sound much like "life, liberty, and the pursuit of happiness." It sounds like a nation of drones.

It's not likely that you can break down your boss's door and demand fewer hours, more vacation, and for him to give you back your life while he's at it. But since everybody's sort of sick of the grind, things may be changing so that these ideas aren't as outside as they used to be.

So the first step in planning how to balance your life and your work is to realize that you are not being a selfish, lazy kid just because you don't want to repeat the workaholic eighties. And it doesn't mean you can't be dedicated to your job or truly enthusiastic about doing great work. It just means you want a life—and that's fair.

So how do you go about making sure you've got a good part of your life left once you join the working world? Here are a few ideas:

**When You're Not at Work, Be Inefficient** Some people find that once they start working and get used to planning, scheduling, rushing, and doing, it seeps over into the rest of their life. They can't even have a beer and kill an afternoon watching Godzilla movies, for crying out loud. This happens because work reinforces the value of efficiency. We're so damn efficient these days we don't even realize that other values—like love and fun—used to be (and still can be) more important.

A warning signal is when you start to get the feeling that you're always wasting time—no matter what you do. It smells like this: You try to think of something to do and you say to yourself, "I better hurry up and decide *because I'm wasting time thinking about it.* Oh my God, *I'm wasting time thinking about how I'm wasting time.* I should just *do* something. I could go to the movies—no, there must be something to do that would be *more* fun than that. If I think a little more, I could probably think of the *most efficient* way to have fun, and that way I'd be getting the most fun out of the time I have. But I better hurry up because I'm *wasting time* again. . . ."

Time to chill. You've got to get out of artificial corporate time and back to a connection with the gentle flow of nature's rhythms. Try watching your dog scratch himself for a while.

**Don't let work define who you are.** Remember that when you meet people at work, they'll think of you in terms of work. It takes a tremendous amount of energy for them to think of you in other terms. T. S. Eliot, for example, was working in a bank. A friend of his, the literary critic I. A. Richards, met Eliot's boss on vacation. The boss wanted to know if Richards thought Eliot was a good poet. Richards said yes. The boss thought it was good that Eliot did well at his "hobby" and that it probably helped with his work. The boss gave Richards a piece of information that he said Richards could take back to T. S. Eliot. "I don't see why—in time, of course—he mightn't even become a branch manager."

Think of yourself as a branch manager twenty-four hours a day, and you'll probably never be one of the greatest English poets of the twentieth century. To avoid this, cultivate the other parts of yourself and then let those parts hang out for all to see. If you play bass in a screaming Grunge band at night, don't try to hide that at work. Tell people. It's good for your soul.

And keep a watch out for the qualities in you that are being reinforced by work—they may not be the ones you want. Psychologist LaBier says this:

> Some people find themselves doing work which fits their character orientation, but in a negative way: it supports and strengthens whatever negative traits or irrational attitudes existed within them, but had been dormant. An example would be a lawyer whose obsessive-compulsive tendencies are strengthened by work which requires and rewards those character traits. There is congruency between the person's character and her work. But she does not develop as long as her situation

> supports and makes adaptive her negative side. She may perform well, as long as the environment remains the same. But overall, she suffers as a person. And if the work changes in a way which requires more creative, spontaneous or flexible thinking, she may be in deep trouble.

If your friends start to tell you that you've been acting weird since you took your job, pay attention. They may see something you don't.

**Don't Pretend to Like Work if You Hate It** Go ahead and say it. Say it with me now, "I HATE WORK." There, didn't that feel good? When you had some scummy summer job before your first "real" job and you hated it you probably felt a lot freer about admitting that you hated it. But when you've got your first job in your chosen career, you may think there's something wrong with you unless you love your job. But maybe it's just this job, not your career path, that isn't working. Or maybe it's just that you have to do it for forty hours a week that's got you down. Go ahead and bitch out loud about your job, or at least parts of it. That way you'll also feel better about the parts you do like.

**Don't Pretend to Hate Work if You Like It** A strange and wonderful thing can happen with jobs: you actually like what you do. You have a sudden interest in ball bearings, and it's important and exciting that you're working on the ball bearings that will revolutionize the industry. Sometimes this can be embarrassing. You go to a party and somebody asks you what you do, and you ache to tell them, and you start to, and you suddenly realize you're talking about ball bearings and that you probably sound like a geek. But you've got to face it: you like ball bearings, and there's nothing wrong with that.

If your friends ridicule you because you're job isn't cool enough, you need new friends. The worst thing you can do is clam up and decide not to bring work home with you. That's how we got a generation full of men (mostly) in the 1950s who got ulcers, drank too much, and never explained to their kids what they spent a third of their waking hours doing.

**Stand Up for Something** Business will pressure you to conform. Sometimes to stay sane you have to pick an issue and refuse to conform. LaBier says:

> Some people find that they can develop new values or strengthen others which were weak but important to them by taking a stand on principles at work. This often takes the form of resisting the system in some way, either to maintain a principle which they believe the organization has violated, even at the expense of their career, or to maintain their sanity within what they perceive to be an insane environment.

You might even try picking some advice from this book and intentionally defying it, just for practice. After all, you don't need some book to tell you how to behave at work. Take my words of wisdom from Chapter 3 and stomp on them. "I *will* bring stinky leftovers from home," you say. "I shall zap them in the microwave, eat them in the lunchroom, and read *People* magazine, and I don't care if I never become vice president of this pop stand." If you have trouble letting go of the vice president fantasy, imagine yourself as becoming vice president *in spite* of your lunch *faux pas.* When they profile you in *The Wall Street Journal,* someone will say, "She always brought these stinky leftovers and ate them in the lunchroom with the secretaries. She never lost sight of her connection to the common workers of the company."

**Face the Fear** Do things on purpose that you're afraid of, just to make sure you've got some courage. Go into the boss's office and suggest that the company change its name. I did that once. I walked into the *president's* office and suggested what I thought was a better name. He looked at me like I was pretty weird, but the ground didn't open up and swallow me or anything. He just told me to talk it over with my boss, which I already knew was his way of saying forget it.

**Think of Work as Your Day Job** This is the L.A. trick. "I'm not really a traffic clerk, I'm really a screenwriter/actor/director although right now I'm waiting on tables" is not a bad way to psych yourself through another day of work. A day job doesn't have to be drudge work. It might help to think of it as satisfying only one dimension of your multifaceted personality—and that can be a pretty important part.

In the 1970s, there was a guy who worked at Polaroid named Tom Scholz. He got pretty high up in the company—he was a senior product designer—so you can guess there was something about his job he liked for him to put that much into it. But he never gave up another part of his ambition, and that was to write and play music. Eventually he sent his homemade tape into Epic Records, and they signed him and his group—Boston. Epic simply reworked his tapes, resulting in the fastest-selling debut album in rock history. Scholz's dream became a record that sold 6 1/2 million copies.

**Learn About Other Stuff** No matter how much you're interested in what you do, learn about something else or you'll bore everyone you know and eventually you'll bore yourself. Because reading is a part of just about everybody's job, it's easy to get in the habit of only reading work stuff. If you have time to read, you feel like you should always be reading something for work. Forget that! Read something else once in a while.

**Friends and Family** For more than ninety-nine percent of the time humans have been on earth we've lived in tribal groups of no more than thirty-five people. We've evolved to live in groups like that; small communities of family and friends—not small groups of workers, and not in multilevel hierarchies. Our emotions are gauged to handle that kind of group. If you rely on work to give you all your satisfaction—or even most of it—you're barking up the wrong evolutionary tree. Hang with your friends and family, and let work go.

## When Work Works

I've tried to be straight with you through this whole book. If something about the working world sucks, I've tried to say that. It may seem like I've spent most of the book on what's wrong, but that's because that's the stuff you need to deal with.

So, for the record, let me tell you that work can be very cool. It's like making a good movie. You've heard all the crap that goes on in Hollywood: backbiting, exploitation, money-grubbing. And some people would say that that's all there is to the movie business.

But those are just the obstacles—and there are obstacles to anything worth doing. The high comes when you see all the obstacles—every stinking one—and you knock 'em down, one at a time. You roll over one, you duck under the next, and you never stop to complain that God should've made the world different. She didn't, and that's it. And when the obstacles are behind you and you sail into the clear blue of a project that kicks, you get a feeling that can only be described as *yes*. And it doesn't matter if it's Jurassic Park or the best damn ball bearings the world has ever seen. What's important is that it's good, and that you did it. And that feels great.

So get out there and kick it.

# Index